D0596253

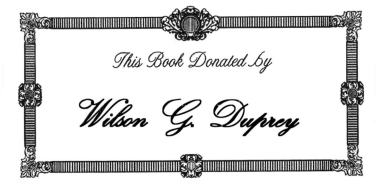

*This Book Donated by*

*Wilson G. Duprey*

# British Library
# Reference Division

# Guide to the Department of Oriental Manuscripts and Printed Books

Compiled by
H. J. Goodacre and A. P. Pritchard

Published for
The British Library
by
British Museum Publications Limited

© 1977, The British Library Board 🔲🔲
ISBN 0 7141 0658 5
Published by British Museum Publications Ltd.
6 Bedford Square London WC1B 3RA

On 1 July 1973, the Library collections of
The British Museum were transferred to
The British Library Board.

Designed by Harry Green
Set in 10 on 11 point Imprint by Tradespools Ltd., Frome, Somerset
Printed in Great Britain at the University Press, Oxford
by Vivian Ridler Printer to the University

# Contents

# List of Plates

# Foreword

The Department of Oriental Manuscripts and Printed Books is responsible for the British Library's collections in the humanities and social and political sciences in the languages of Asia and North and North-east Africa. Western language materials relating to these regions are, for the most part, in other Departments and the overall coverage is outlined in A. Gaur: 'Oriental Material in the Reference Division of the British Library' (*British Library Journal*, vol. 2, No. 2, 1976).

From 1838 onwards catalogues of individual language collections have been published, the advantage of this system being that scholars specializing in particular language areas have a conspectus of their materials presented and analysed in terms related to their study with the inclusion of titles in the original script in each catalogue. The difficulties have been the proliferation of separate volumes and the absence for certain languages of recent or indeed any published catalogues.

The present work is accordingly aimed at representing the collections as a whole with reference both to published and unpublished catalogues and should greatly facilitate access to them. A Committee was set up in 1972 and I should like to thank all who served on it with me as well as many members of the Department, including the language specialists who have written about their own sections and the staff concerned with public services. Special thanks are due to Mr Phylip Pritchard who was responsible for the introductory material and the general bibliographies and to Mr Hugh Goodacre, upon whom devolved the greater part of the co-ordination and editing of contributions. Our thanks are also due to Mr K. B. Gardner and Mr. J. Losty of this Department and to Mr P. A. Clayton, the Managing Editor of British Museum Publications Ltd., for their advice and help in the later stages of editing and production.

G. E. Marrison
Director and Keeper

# Introduction

## HISTORY

Before 1867 Oriental manuscripts and printed books in the British Museum were incorporated in the Departments of Manuscripts and of Printed Books respectively. By the mid-nineteenth century, however, this arrangement was proving to be less than satisfactory. The Oriental manuscripts numbered about 7000 separate volumes by 1866 and there was every anticipation, substantiated by subsequent events, of considerable additions to the manuscript collections, especially in Arabic, Persian and Sanskrit. At a meeting of the Trustees of the British Museum on 11 October 1866, John Winter Jones (1805–81), the Principal Librarian, believing that 'the study of Oriental languages is the labour of a life and could not be successfully pursued by one who at the same time gave his attention properly to European manuscripts', raised the question of the expediency of placing a portion of the contents of the Department of Manuscripts under a separate Keeper, the Keeper of Oriental Manuscripts. In a meeting later that same month, Winter Jones broached the subject once more, on this occasion outlining proposals for the suggested constitution of a Department of Oriental Manuscripts. Since by this time a nucleus of Oriental specialists already existed in the British Museum, there was to be no recruitment of staff from outside the establishment. The Department of Oriental Manuscripts was to be under the charge of a Keeper but was to remain a sub-division of the Department of Manuscripts, and its expenses were to continue to form part of the annual estimates of the Keeper of Manuscripts. The Keeper of Oriental Manuscripts was to be responsible for the purchase, cataloguing and arrangement of the Oriental manuscripts but where these manuscripts formed part of the foundation collections of the British Museum, they were to be described in the Oriental catalogues without necessarily being removed from the custody of the Keeper of (Western) Manuscripts. The first, and only, Keeper of the new Department was Charles Rieu (1820–1902) who had come to the British Museum in 1847 as a Supernumerary Assistant in the Department of Manuscripts and who, during his long term of office as Keeper, produced important catalogues of the Arabic, Persian and Turkish collections.

One of the first to work on the oriental manuscripts and printed books in the British Museum was Charles Godfrey Woide (1725–90), more widely known as the editor of the New Testament of the *Codex Alexandrinus*, who, besides being in charge of the Hebrew and Arabic manuscripts, was an early scholar in the field of Coptic studies. Other notable scholars of the early period were Thomas Maurice (1754–1824) who worked on the Indian collections; Friedrich August Rosen (1805–37) and Josiah Forshall (1795–1863);

Joseph Zedner (1804–71) who was a pioneer in the field of Hebrew biblio-graphy; William Cureton (1801–64) who was responsible for much of the early work carried out on the Syriac and Arabic manuscripts; Duncan Forbes (1798–1868) who, in 1849, began to catalogue the Persian manuscripts; James Fuller Blumhardt (d. 1922) who carried out important work on the North Indian languages; Ernst Anton Haas (1835–82) and Cecil Bendall (1856–1906) who did the same for Sanskrit and related languages; and Sir Robert Kennaway Douglas (1838–1913) who produced what is believed to have been the first catalogue in Europe to list the holdings of a large library of Chinese printed books, manuscripts and drawings.

The formation of a separate department to administer both manuscripts and printed books in oriental languages had been advocated since at least 1850 but it was not until 1891 that the Trustees of the British Museum gained the Treasury's approval to establish a Department of Oriental Printed Books and Manuscripts. This Department was to come into operation on the retire-ment of Dr Rieu on 1 January 1892. As in 1866, this approval was subject to the condition that staff, funds, manuscripts and printed books were to be drawn from the existing departments of the British Museum. Proposals for the organization of the new Department were presented to the Trustees by the Principal Librarian on 9 January 1892 and these were ratified on 9 April of the same year. The Department has continued to function on this basis although it altered its title to Department of Oriental Manuscripts and Printed Books when it became part of the British Library in July 1973, thus reflecting the priority of manuscripts in the history of the Department.

To enumerate all those notable scholars who have served in the Depart-ment since 1892 would prove too lengthy an exercise but the names of those who have held the post of Keeper are indicative of the high standards main-tained by the Department since its inception—Sir Robert Kennaway Douglas (January 1892–March 1908), Lionel David Barnett (April 1908–October 1936), Lionel Giles (November 1936–October 1940), Alexander Strathern Fulton (October 1940–February 1953), Jacob Leveen (February 1953–December 1956), Kenneth Burslam Gardner (July 1957–September 1970), Martin Lings (July 1971–July 1974) and Geoffrey Edward Marrison (No-vember 1974–).

## COLLECTIONS AND CATALOGUES

Most of the British Museum's foundation collections contained some oriental manuscripts and printed books—in the Harleian Collection, for instance, there were many Anglo-Jewish charters, 130 Hebrew, 54 Arabic and 34 Turkish manuscripts, and in the Sloane Collection, 13 Hebrew, 6 Sanskrit and 20 Tamil manuscripts. It was during the nineteenth century, however, that a flood of oriental manuscripts and printed books began to pour into the British Museum. Much of the material was associated with famous collectors of the period and, particularly in the case of manuscripts, parts of the Depart-ment's collections were built up as a result of the acquisition of complete collections, whether by donation, bequest or purchase. Though most of these collections were specialized, some of them, such as that of Claudius James

Rich (1786–1821) and William Erskine (1773–1852) ranged over a number of oriental languages.

Printed catalogues of parts of the oriental collection had appeared even before the creation of the Department of Oriental Manuscripts in 1867. The aim of the first catalogue eventually proved to be too ambitious. In Latin and entitled *Catalogus codicum manuscriptorum orientalium qui in Museo Britannico asservantur*, it was published in three parts between 1838 and 1871 and covered the existing Syriac, Karshuni, Arabic and Ethiopic manuscript collections. Since then separate catalogues for each language or group of languages has been the rule. Between 1867 and 1892, catalogues of the Bengali, Chinese, Ethiopic, Hebrew, Hindustani, Marathi and Gujarati, Persian, Sanskrit and Pali, Syriac, and Turkish material in the Department were produced. The publication of catalogues of a consistently high standard has continued, among the most recent to appear being the late Cyril Moss's catalogue of Syriac books, Albertine Gaur's catalogue of Malayalam books and her catalogue of Indian charters on copper plates.

From the beginning, entries for the catalogues of the Department's acquisitions were handwritten on blue slips and were edited for publication when a sufficient accumulation in a particular language or group of languages had been made. In the case of manuscripts, a complete handwritten accessions list of oriental manuscripts in the Department is maintained in the Oriental Reading Room; this list often includes fairly detailed descriptions of the manuscripts. In addition, a classed inventory lists titles of manuscripts by language, and thus functions as an index volume for the accessions list. Since 1959, current acquisitions of printed books have been catalogued on cards by author, title and, in most cases, subject. As far as possible, the 'blue--slip catalogues' have been eliminated either by publication of printed catalogues or by transfer of the entries on to cards, but there are still some parts of the collections for which the blue-slip catalogues are the only available documentation. The Department also contributes entries for newly acquired books to the *Union Catalogue of Asian Publications* edited at the School of Oriental and African Studies, University of London.

## SCOPE OF THE DEPARTMENT'S COLLECTIONS AND WORK
Over 200 different languages are represented in the collections, comprising nearly all the languages of Asia, and most of the languages of North and North-east Africa, insofar as they incorporate a long literary tradition. Chronologically the collections span the period from Chinese oracle bones of the Shang period (second millennium BC) to current publications from the whole of Asia and North Africa.

Assessment of the strengths of the various manuscripts collections may be found in the appropriate sections, but mention may be made here of the artistic richness of the whole collection. This is an emphasis lacking in the printed manuscript catalogues, but which during this century has become more prominent as the artistic heritage of the oriental peoples has received its due recognition first by Western scholarship and then by the educated public. Some of the material is either mainly European (the exquisite illuminated Hebrew codices from medieval Germany, France, Italy, Spain and Portugal), or derives its artistic form to some extent from Byzantium (the manuscripts of the eastern Churches in Syriac, Coptic, Armenian and Ethiopic). The Islamic art of calligraphy and illumination was also recognized early for its intrinsic value, and the Department's collections contain splendid examples from all over the Islamic world—Moorish Spain, Morocco, Egypt, the Middle East, Persia, Afghanistan and India. The recognition of the value of oriental paintings came much later, though the Museum had been building up its collections. Today the Department has a superb collection of Persian and Persian-based painting, from Persia (the court styles of Baghdad, Shiraz, Herat, Tabriz, Qazwin, Isfahan, as well as the provincial styles), India (imperial Mughal manuscripts from the 1580s through to the nineteenth century, provincial Mughal, the Deccan, Panjab and Kashmir), and Turkey. The collections also include outstanding examples of the art of Buddhist and Hindu India and South-east Asia on palm-leaf, bark, cloth and paper; from India proper are represented the Pala and Nepalese schools, the Jain style, Rajput schools (particularly rich in Mewar), the regional schools of Assam, Orissa, and Kashmir; from Tibet illustrated manuscripts and *tankas*; from Burma and Thailand lavishly painted folding-books, and illustrated palm-leaf manuscripts from Java and Bali. From the Far East come many fine examples of Chinese and Japanese calligraphy and painting, as well as large collections of early block-printed books which reproduce faithfully the art of the calligrapher and ink-painter.

The Department's importance for scholarship and research does not rest only on its collections of rare and beautiful manuscripts written in past ages. It is also a modern working library of printed books, serving the needs of the research scholar in all fields of study relating to the people and countries of Asia and North Africa. Year by year its collections increase as more and more books pour from the printing presses of these once-remote parts of the world. It is one of the most fundamental and responsible tasks of the language and area specialists on the staff of the Department to select those books which are of research value and will stand the test of time. Reaching out beyond the traditional fields of study such as Islamic theology, Hebrew rabbinical studies, Sanskrit literature and Confucian philosophy, the Department also collects widely in all branches of the humanities and in the social sciences such as law, politics, economics, sociology and every topic that touches human society today.

Oriental works in the field of modern science and technology are the responsibility of the Science Reference Library, but traditional science and technology of all periods and the history of sciences in the Orient are represented by large collections in this Department. Printed books and journals in western languages on oriental subjects are kept in the Department of Printed Books but can be transferred on request to the Oriental Reading Room if required for use in conjunction with the Department's own oriental material.

Government publications are available in the Official Publications Library. This class of material was formerly handled by the Department of Printed Books. Since the independence of many countries of Asia and Africa in the present century, indigenous languages have been increasingly used for official publications. To acquire and process this material, an Oriental Exchange Unit was set up which, in 1975, was transferred to the Department of Oriental Manuscripts and Printed Books. These collections cover many of the languages of Asia and North Africa and are specially strong in Japanese and Arabic language materials.

The Department of Manuscripts has western language materials of oriental interest, including large collections of papers and documents related to the presence of Europeans in Asia and Africa. Printed and manuscript maps of oriental regions are kept in the Map Library but some maps in manuscript and early printed form, most of which are in oriental languages, are also to be found in the Department of Oriental Manuscripts and Printed Books. Separate miniature paintings, some taken from illuminated oriental manuscripts, are kept in the Department of Oriental Antiquities of the British Museum. Printed oriental music in western notation is kept in the Music Library. Although works of oriental scholarship in western languages are held, as a general rule, by the Department of Printed Books, the Department of Oriental Manuscripts and Printed Books has its own copies of most of the major reference works, especially bibliographical items, needed by the orientalist regardless of language.

Current acquisition policy aims at maintaining a comprehensive library of writings in the indigenous languages of Asia and North Africa, collecting Oriental documents not only for their actual content, though this is of primary importance, but also for their material form, as illustrating on the one hand the history of the written word, and on the other the development of the book in all its varieties. The arts of calligraphy, illumination and binding, and examples of the various methods of printing receive increasing attention. In modern times there has been an inevitable diminution in the acquisition of manuscripts as the sources of supply dried up. This factor, coupled with the enormous expansion of publication in Asia, has increased the proportion of time spent on printed books in the Department's work. The Department now has about 40,000 manuscripts and 400,000 printed books.

Its staff includes specialists in the languages and cultures of the regions covered by the Department: their work goes beyond the normal library tasks of acquisition, cataloguing and provision for research workers, since they are engaged in research on the collections and in providing a service of consultation, interpretation and bibliographical information. The work of these specialists also includes the study of writing materials, the many varied scripts, decoration, illustration and binding as well as purely textual studies. Also a part of their work is the exhibition of the Department's collections. Some of the finest manuscripts and printed books are always on display in the twelve cases at the south end of the King's Library, and from time to time a larger display is put out, for which a printed catalogue may be prepared.

## READER SERVICES
### Oriental Reading Room
The Oriental Reading Room, situated on the ground floor, offers facilities to

all research students and to all members of the public with a serious interest in the collections who wish to work on them. There is accommodation for 26 readers. Opening hours are Monday–Friday from 10 a.m. until 4.45 p.m. and on Saturday from 10 a.m. until 12.45 p.m. The Department and the Reading Room are closed on New Year's Day, Good Friday, Christmas Day and Boxing Day, and the Reading Room during the third week of October each year. Admission to the Oriental Reading Room is by ticket only. Tickets are of two types: long-term passes (for which application is to be made in the Oriental Reading Room) are issued from the Readers' Admission Office; temporary tickets are issued by the Reading Room staff and are valid for a period of not more than six days.

The Oriental Reading Room is administered by the Superintendent assisted by clerical staff and library assistants. The clerical staff deal with requests for manuscripts and printed books and general queries from readers and the public. If the assistance required is beyond the scope of the clerical staff, the necessary specialist staff are then consulted. Since the Department's collections are not on open access—except for standard reference works— application forms for the requisition of the manuscripts and printed books are available in the Reading Room. The required material is then collected from the storage areas and brought to readers by the library assistants. Readers are not allowed to remove manuscripts or printed books from the Oriental Reading Room.

One of the services provided by the Department is the examination, identification and appraisal of objects, manuscripts and printed matter which are brought from time to time by members of the public. Such articles are accepted by the Reading Room staff; an official receipt is given, and the deposit is forwarded to the specialist staff who then communicate directly with the depositor. The only proviso is that members of the Department cannot accept liability for the opinions they may express on material submitted for identification or for information, nor can they give valuations or translations.

There is a microfilm and a microfiche reader in the Reading Room. An ultra-violet reader in the Department of Manuscripts can be used by special arrangement if required. Photographic orders may be handed in to the Reading Room staff.

**Photographic Services**

Photographs of manuscripts and printed material in the Department's collections can be provided subject to the Department's approval and to the provisions of the laws of copyright. Processes available are black and white prints; colour transparencies; 35mm slides; ektachrome transparencies; ektacolour prints; lantern slides; ultra-violet and infra-red photographs; microfilms (microfilming has been discontinued for manuscripts containing miniatures or illuminations); photocopies; and electrostatic (xerox) copying. No 'rapid-copying' of manuscripts and newspapers is allowed and possible damage to printed books is assessed before rapid-copying is approved. In such cases an alternative type of photography may be suggested.

Further enquiries about the photographic services should be directed to the Department's Photographic Officer.

## BINDING AND CONSERVATION

For the binding and repair of manuscripts and printed books, the services of
HMSO Bindery are used. The Department also has the services of an ex-
perienced furbisher whose task it is to treat deteriorating leather bindings
and carry out other such essential repairs. The entire manuscript collection
is so treated every three years.

The Department has its own Conservation workshop whose officers are
primarily responsible for the repair and preservation of various classes of
oriental materials not usually handled in Western libraries. These include
oriental paper, textiles, palm-leaf, bark, papyrus, various skins, wood, bone,
ivory and metal. The work also includes restoration and conservation of
illuminated manuscripts. The conservation officers advise on the maintenance
and proper storage conditions of the collections and deal with any emergencies
which arise in this area. They also play a major role in the preparation of
material to be shown in exhibitions organized by the Department. Besides
acting as consultants to specialists and the public, the conservation officers
are continually engaged in research into new processes for the preservation,
*etc*, of oriental materials, and in many instances the results of their investiga-
tions are adopted as standard practice by other libraries and institutions in the
field of conservation throughout the world.

## BIBLIOGRAPHY

Minutes of the meetings of the Trustees of the British Museum for the years
      1866 and 1891–1892.
BRITISH MUSEUM. *Annual report of the general progress of the Museum and of the
      British Museum — Natural History — for the year 1921 (–1938)*. London
      1922–39.
      Reports for the previous years were issued as Parliamentary Papers.
BRITISH MUSEUM. *Report of the Trustees*. London 1967; in progress. The
      report for 1966 also covers the period up to the last pre-war Annual report.
BRITISH MUSEUM. *The British Museum. A guide to its public services*. Second
      edition. London 1970. pp. 44–47.
COLLISON, R. L. W. *Directory of libraries and special collections on Asia and
      North Africa . . . With the assistance of Brenda E. Moon*. Crosby Lockwood,
      London 1970. pp. 45–47.
ESDAILE, A. *The British Museum Library*. Allen and Unwin, London 1946.
      pp. 294–321.
ESDAILE, A. *National libraries of the world . . . Second edition, completely revised
      by F. J. Hill*. Library Association, London 1957. pp. 17–18.
FRANCIS, F. C. *The catalogues of the British Museum. 3. Oriental Printed Books
      and Manuscripts. Revised edition*. London 1959.
GARDNER, K. B., and others. The Department of Oriental Printed Books and
      Manuscripts of the British Museum. In: *Journal of Asian Studies*, 18
      (1959), pp. 310–18.
GAUR, A. Oriental material in the Reference Division of the British Library.
      In: *British Library Journal*, Vol. 2. No. 2. Besides reference to this Depart-
      ment, also includes reference to the Department of (Western) Manuscripts,

the Department of Printed Books, the Map Library, the Music Library, the Official Publications Library, and the Science Reference Library.

GAUR, A. Oriental Printed Books and Manuscripts. In: *Treasures of the British Museum*, edited by F. C. Francis. Thames and Hudson, London 1971. pp. 238–60.

HOSKING, R. F. and MEREDITH-OWENS, G. M. *Handbook of Asian scripts*. London 1966.
An exhibition catalogue.

LOSTY, J., ed. *Oriental manuscripts*. London 1973.
An exhibition catalogue.

MILLER, E. *That Noble Cabinet : A History of the British Museum*. Andre Deutsch, London 1973.
With extensive bibliography.

PEARSON, J. D. *Oriental and Asian bibliography. An introduction with some reference to Africa*. Crosby Lockwood, London 1966. pp. 164–70.

PEARSON, J. D. *Oriental manuscripts in Europe and North America—a survey*. Interdocumentation Co, Zug 1971.

PRITCHARD, P. Index of articles in the *British Museum Quarterly* on material in the Department of Oriental Manuscripts and Printed Books. In: *British Library Journal*, Vol. 2. No. 2.

THOMPSON, J. R. F. The Rich manuscripts. In: *British Museum Quarterly*, XXVII (1963), pp. 18–23.

# Language Sections

The Department's collections are described below in alphabetical order of language within four main geographical areas as follows: NEAR AND MIDDLE EAST (with North and North East Africa and Muslim Spain, and Turcic and Iranian languages of Central Asia), SOUTH ASIA, SOUTH EAST ASIA (with Polynesia and Madagascar), FAR EAST.

In these language sections, all the Department's catalogues, published and unpublished, have been included. These catalogues fall into the following categories:

### Published catalogues
A complete set of these is on open access in the Oriental Reading Room. Information on those which are in print is available in *Books in Print*, the periodic catalogue of British Museum Publications Ltd. Unless otherwise indicated, all published catalogues with a London imprint referred to in the following language sections were published by the Trustees of the British Museum, or by British Museum Publications Ltd., for the British Library Board.

### Blue-slip catalogues
These are maintained by the language specialists, who should be consulted for further information.

### Card catalogues
A complete set of card catalogues is on open access in the Reading Room.

### Typescript and handwritten catalogues and lists
Copies of all such items are on open access in the Reading Room.

### Classed inventory and List of oriental manuscripts
The List of oriental manuscripts is a complete handwritten accessions list of oriental manuscripts in the Department, and often includes fairly detailed descriptions. The Classed inventory lists titles only, arranged by language; it thus functions as a language index to the complete List. In the following language sections, these items are referred to collectively as 'Classed inventory'. They are kept on open access in the Reading Room.

Besides describing the Department's catalogues, the language sections also include references to publications by other agencies which include or comprise lists, catalogues or other directly relevant bibliographical information on the Department's collections. Publications by the Department are included even when they do not fall within these categories.

In the case of the major collections it is, of course, not feasible to provide anything but an outline bibliography; however, in the case of minor collections, it has usually been possible to give more comprehensive treatment.

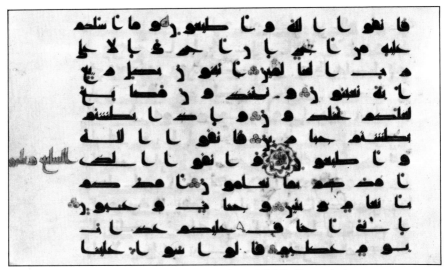

**1 Arabic.** Page from a Kufic Qur'ān on vellum. Middle East, ninth century.
Or. 1397, f. 13a.

# Near and Middle East

The principal collections from these regions include the literature of (1) *Judaism*, with manuscripts of oriental provenance and from medieval Europe, and printed books from Israel, Europe, America and elsewhere; (2) *Christianity*, of the Oriental Churches, in Arabic, Syriac, Coptic, Ethiopic, Armenian and Georgian languages as well as secular materials of Soviet provenance and (3) *Islam*, with materials from South West Asia, Central Asia, North Africa and Muslim Spain in Arabic, Persian, Turkish and other languages.

## AMHARIC
*MSS. about 50 ; PB approaching 1000.*
The manuscripts include biblical and patristic translations, philogical, medical, magical and chronographical works and letters (including some by Kings Tewodros II and John). Besides, in the headings, colophons, marginalia and flyleaf inscriptions of many Ethiopic manuscripts there are dedication notes, etc., in Amharic providing source material for monastic, ecclesiastic, court and social history. There are also some important early specimens of written Amharic.

The printed books cover the whole range of Ge'ez and general literature, and include a good selection of early and current secular prose and several early periodicals. Of the early editions printed in Ethiopia, there are nearly thirty of which no copy is known at Addis Ababa or Rome.

**For manuscripts, see:**
DILLMANN, A. *Catalogus codicum manuscriptorum qui in Museo Britannico asservantur. Pars tertia, codices aethiopicos amplectens.* London 1847. pp. 90.
Includes 15 items wholly or partly in Amharic.
WRIGHT, W. *Catalogue of the Ethiopic manuscripts in the British Museum acquired since the year 1847.* London 1877. pp. 379; pl. 13.
Includes at least a further 10 items wholly or partly in Amharic.
STRELCYN, S. *Catalogue of Ethiopic manuscripts in the British Library acquired since 1878.* London 1976.
Includes 25 Amharic items. With an index of titles, authors and place-names; an index of owners and scribes; a chronological list; and a list of the Amharic items.

**For printed books, see:**
*Card catalogue of Amharic books.*

## ARABIC
*MSS. 6000 ; PB 30,000.*
There were 166 Arabic manuscripts in the foundation collections, to which were added 31 brought back from Egypt in 1802 after the Battle of the Nile.

The first substantial acquisition of Arabic manuscripts, however, was the purchase, in 1825, of the Rich collection, which included about 400 Arabic items. The rest of the nineteenth century saw the acquisition of many other collections. The Hodgson, Yule, St Sternschuss, Barker, Lynch and Cureton collections are included in the first catalogue. In the period from 1865 to the publication of the supplementary catalogue of 1894, six more important collections were added, namely those of Jaba, Murray, Rawlinson, von Kremer, Glaser and Lane. Acquisition of Arabic manuscripts remains relatively high to the present day.

The manuscript collection includes many unsurpassed specimens of Arabic calligraphy and illumination and probably the oldest Quran manuscript in Europe. It also includes a large number of unique or autograph copies, and is in general one of the most important primary sources for Arabic and Islamic studies.

The collection of printed books is also comprehensive, beginning with a fine collection of early European editions, including the earliest Arabic printed book. *See also* KARSHUNI. For Judaeo-Arabic, *see* HEBREW.

**For manuscripts, see:**

CURETON, W. and RIEU, C. *Catalogus codicum manuscriptorum orientalium qui in Museo Britannico asservantur. Pars secunda, codices arabicos amplectens.* London 1846–71. pp. 888.

About 2000 items. Cureton's catalogue, pp. 1–352 of this volume, was published in two parts in 1846 and 1852, the second part having been largely revised by Rieu. The latter subsequently added a supplement and four appendices which almost doubled the volume of the book. A complete edition of this work in one volume was ultimately published in 1871. With indexes of personal names, titles, and subjects.

RIEU, C. *Supplement to the catalogue of the Arabic manuscripts in the British Museum.* London 1894. pp. 953.

About 1500 items. With indexes of titles, persons' names and subjects.

ELLIS, A. G. and EDWARDS, E. *Descriptive list of the Arabic manuscripts acquired by the Trustees of the British Museum since 1894.* London 1912. pp. 120.

About 900 items. With indexes of titles and of persons.

*Classed inventory.* Includes about 1800 Arabic items acquired since 1912.

*Blue-slip catalogue of Arabic manuscripts acquired since 1912.*

**See also:**

FULTON, A. S., ed. Facsimile of the manuscript of *al-Kitāb al-bāri' fī l-luḡah* by Ismāʿīl ibn al-Qāsim al-Qālī. Published by the Trustees of the British Museum. London 1933. pp. 166.

A facsimile of Or. 9811.

**For printed books, see:**

ELLIS, A. G. *Catalogue of Arabic books in the British Museum.* Vols. 1–2. London 1894–1901. Vol. 3. Indexes by A. S. Fulton. London 1935. Vols. 1–3 reprinted 1967.

About 8000 items.

FULTON, A. S. and ELLIS, A. G. *Supplementary catalogue of Arabic printed books in the British Museum.* London 1926. pp. 6; cols. 1188.
About 5000 items acquired 1901–1926. With indexes of titles, subjects, and alternative forms of personal names.

FULTON, A. S. and LINGS, M. *Second supplementary catalogue of Arabic printed books in the British Museum, 1927–1957.* London 1959. pp. ix, cols. 1132.
About 4500 items. With indexes of titles and of subjects.

LINGS, M. and SAFADI, Y. H. *Third supplementary catalogue of Arabic printed books in the British Library 1958–1969.* London 1976. 4 vols.
About 9000 items. Vols. 1–2. Authors. Vol. 3. Titles. Vol. 4. Subjects.

*Blue-slip catalogue of Arabic printed books acquired since 1970.*

## ARMENIAN

*MSS. 172 ; PB 6000.*
Some of the manuscript items came with the foundation and other early collections. They include some finely illuminated volumes.

**For manuscripts, see:**

CONYBEARE, F. C. *Catalogue of Armenian manuscripts in the British Museum, to which is appended a catalogue of Georgian manuscripts in the British Museum* by J. O. Wardrop. London 1913. pp. 424.
Describes 149 items. With indexes of names of persons, places, and subjects.

*Classed inventory.* Includes 23 Armenian items acquired since 1914.

**For printed books, see:**

*Blue-slip catalogue of Armentian books.* About 6000 items.

## COPTIC

*MSS. over 1500 ; PB about 300.*
The manuscript collection includes a wide range of texts on papyrus, leather, parchment and paper. An early acquisition (1785) was a Gnostic work, the *Pistis Sophia.* The bulk of the collection, however, was assembled through Wallis Budge who acquired a large share of the library of the White Monastery of Shenoute at Athribis, as well as much material from the monasteries of the Wadi Natrun and the Fayyum. Important subsequent additions were: the documents found at Aphrodito in 1901; the codices brought from Edfu by Rustafjaell in 1907; legal papyri from Jême; the Curzon collection, which included the famous *Gospel Catena* of AD 889, grammars and glossaries in Arabic, and further works of Shenoute; and the Wadi Sarga fragments.

**For manuscripts, see:**

CRUM, W. E. *Catalogue of the Coptic manuscripts in the British Museum.* London 1905. pp. 648; pl. 15.
1252 entries. Arranged by subject within main divisions according to dialect. With indexes of Biblical passages, personal names, place names, Greek words, Coptic words, Arabic names and words, and subjects. [T. Orlandi of Milan has in the press a contribution to *Le Museon* in which

**2 Coptic.** Leaf from a Bible on papyrus. Egypt, AD 300–350. Or. 7594, f. 53b.

he has listed all the manuscripts not in Crum with comprehensive bibliographies.]

CRUM, W. E., ed. [Coptic texts.] In: *Greek papyri in the British Museum.* Vol.
IV. *The Aphrodito papyri.* Edited by H. I. Bell. *With an appendix of Coptic
papyri edited by W. E. Crum.* London 1910.
152 items, pp. 433–525.
*Classed inventory.* Includes about 200 items not described by Crum.

HYVERNAT, H. Coptic literature. In: *The Catholic Encyclopaedia.* Vol. 16.
New York 1914. pp. 27–30.
Lists the items not described by Crum.

CURZON, R. *Catalogue of materials for writing, early writings on tablets and
stones, rolled and other manuscripts and oriental manuscript books in the
library of the Honourable Robert Curzon.* London 1849. pp. 43; plates.
See pp. 26–28.

DE RUSTAFJAELL, R. *The light of Egypt.* London 1909. pp. 101–38; pls. 39–48.
Items from Edfu.

**For illuminated manuscripts, see:**

BUCHTHAL, H. and KURZ, O. *Hand list of illuminated oriental Christian
manuscripts.* London 1942. pp. 120.
Includes 31 of the Department's Coptic items.

**For printed books, see:**

*Blue-slip catalogue of Coptic books acquired before 1972.* About 1500 slips
    describing some 400 books, of which over 100 are in the Department of
    Printed Books.

*Card catalogue of Coptic books acquired since 1972.* Most Coptic books are also
    entered in the catalogues of the Department of Printed Books.

## ETHIOPIC

*MSS. about 600 ; PB about 1500. Both figures include Amharic, Tigrinya and
other Ethiopian languages.*

The first substantial acquisition of Ethiopic manuscripts was the donation by
the Church of England Missionary Society of 74 codices collected in the
1830s and 1840s by Isenberg and Krapf. Further acquisitions included 349
volumes from Magdala, acquired in 1870. Twelve Ethiopic volumes in the
Curzon collection were acquired later, and 18 items donated by the Well-
come Foundation in 1961 and 1970.

   This Department and the Department of Printed Books between them
hold copies of nearly all the sixteenth and seventeenth century Ethiopic
printed books.

   There is also a comprehensive collection of texts in, and grammars and
lexicons of, Ethiopic and other languages of Ethiopia, namely Tigrinya, Tigre
and other vernaculars of the Semitic, Cushitic and Nilotic groups. For
references to individual languages, *see* INDEX OF LANGUAGES. *See also:*
AMHARIC.

**For manuscripts, see:**

DILLMAN, A. *Catalogus codicum manuscriptorum qui in Museo Britannico
    asservantur. Pars tertia, codices aethiopicos amplectens.* London 1847. pp. 90.
    Describes 78 Ethiopic items, including 4 wholly and 11 partly in Amharic.

WRIGHT, W. *Catalogue of the Ethiopic manuscripts in the British Museum
    acquired since the year 1847.* London 1877. pp. 379; pl. 13.
    408 entries, describing 388 volumes, including about 10 items wholly or
    partly in Amharic.

STRELCYN, S. *Catalogue of Ethiopian manuscripts in the British Library
    acquired since 1878.* London 1976.
    Describes 108 items, including 25 in Amharic. With an index of titles,
    authors and place-names; an index of owners and scribes; a chronological
    list; and a list of the Amharic items.

STRELCYN, S. Les manuscrits éthiopiens de quelques bibliothèques euro-
    péennes décrits récemment. In: *IV Congresso Internazionale di Studi
    Etiopici.* Rome 1964.
    Includes a brief general survey of the items in the above catalogue.

CONTI ROSSINI, C. Manoscritti ed opere abissine in Europa. In: *Rendiconti
    della Reale Accademia dei Lincei.* Vol. VIII (1899), pp. 606–37.
    An analysis of the manuscripts catalogued by Dillman and Wright.

PANKHURST, R. J. The library of the Emperor Tewodros II at Mäqdäla.
    Typescript. Addis Ababa 1971.

**For illuminated items, see:**
*List of illustrated Ethiopic manuscripts.* Typescript. A numerical list.
*Catalogue and subject index of illuminations and miniatures in Ethiopic manuscripts.* In preparation by N. M. Titley.
BUCHTHAL, H. and KURZ, O. *Hand list of illuminated oriental Christian manuscripts.* London 1942. pp. 120.
    Includes 10 Ethiopic items of the fifteenth century in the Department.
HOSKING, F. R. *Ethiopian manuscript painting.* London 1968.
    A wallet of 15 colour transparencies with commentary.
LEROY, J. L'évangeliaire éthiopien illustré du British Museum (Or. 510) et ses sources iconographiques. In: *Annales d' Éthiopie,* 4 (1961), pp. 155–65; pl. XLIV–LIII.
LEROY, J. *Ethiopian painting in the late Middle Ages and under the Gondar Dynasty.* London 1967. pp. 60; pl. 61.
**For printed books, see:**
*Card catalogue of Ethiopic printed books.*

## GEORGIAN AND OTHER CAUCASIAN LANGUAGES

*MSS. 8; PB over 2500, the latter figure including items in other languages concerned with Georgian literature.*

The manuscripts include an important eleventh-century parchment codex on the lives of the saints copied by 'Black John' of the Monastery of the Holy Cross in Jerusalem.

The printed books span the Tsarist and Soviet periods, and also include émigré publications; the emphasis throughout is on the humanities.

In addition to Georgian items, the Department also has a few items in the following Caucasian languages: Kartvelian languages; Svanian and Mingrelo-Laz (these two languages being related to Georgian); Daghestanian languages (a separate group in North-east Caucasus); Circassian (North-west Caucasus); and Abkhazian, another important Caucasian language.

**For manuscripts, see:**
WARDROP, J. O. *Catalogue of Georgian manuscripts in the British Museum.* An appendix to: *Catalogue of Armenian manuscripts in the British Museum* by F. C. Conybeare. London 1913. pp. 424.
    Describes 6 items.
*Classed inventory.* Includes 2 items subsequently acquired. Entitled *Baramiani* and *Omaiani,* both are poetical works.
**For printed books, see:**
LANG, D. M. *Catalogue of the Georgian and other Caucasian printed books in the British Museum.* London 1962. pp. 11; cols. 430.
    Over 1500 items. The first attempt to provide scholars outside the Soviet Union with a working guide to this important branch of world literature.
*Blue-slip catalogue of Georgian and other Caucasian printed books acquired by the British Library since 1962.* Over 1000 items.

## HEBREW

*MSS. about 3000 volumes containing over 5500 works, and about 10,000 Genizah fragments ; PB about 40,000.*

Hebrew manuscripts, several of them finely illuminated, were to be found in most of the foundation collections. The number of manuscripts continued

**3 Hebrew.** Page from the Book of Leviticus, from a MS. of the Pentateuch on vellum. Middle East, early tenth century. Or. 4445, f. 98a.

to grow steadily, but the scope of the collection remained limited; by the
mid-nineteenth century nearly half of the items were biblical codices. During
the latter half of the century, however, the nature of the collection changed
and became more comprehensive. In 1865 the Almanzi library, which included over 300 manuscripts, was purchased. Between 1877 and 1882, nearly
300 manuscripts, mostly Yemenite and Karaite, were bought from the dealer
Shapira. The Department's last major acquisition of Hebrew and Samaritan
manuscripts was the Gaster collection, which came in 1925. Today the Department houses one of the most representative collections of Hebrew
manuscripts in the world.

The only Hebrew printed book in the foundation collections came from
the Old Royal Library of George II. This was the *editio princeps* of the
Babylonian Talmud (Venice 1520–23) which had once belonged to Henry
VIII. In 1759 Solomon da Costa presented 180 printed volumes of rabbinical
literature, most of them of great antiquarian value. The existing collection
was greatly strengthened by the purchase in 1848 of the library of H. J.
Michael of Hamburg, which included 4420 printed books. Today the Department has about 100 Hebrew incunabula and an almost complete collection of
sixteenth century printed books. Many of the items in the collection are
unique. Current acquisition policy covers all aspects of Hebrew literature.

## For manuscripts, see:

MARGOLIOUTH, G. *Catalogue of the Hebrew and Samaritan manuscripts in the
British Museum*. London 1899–1935. 4 vols. Vols. 1–3 reprinted 1965.
> Vols. 1–3. 1206 Hebrew entries, including 30 charters. Vol. 4, by J.
> Leveen, contains an introduction, indexes and a supplementary list of
> manuscripts. Samaritan manuscripts were never in fact included.

MARGOLIOUTH, G., ed. *Descriptive list of Hebrew and Samaritan manuscripts
in the British Museum*. London 1893. pp. 138.
> The entries for Hebrew manuscripts were subsequently superseded in the
> Margoliouth catalogue of 1899–1935. The entries for Samaritan items
> have not, however, been superseded.
> *List of Hebrew, Aramaic, and Arabic Manuscripts believed to be derived
> from the Cairo Genizah* [the Arabic being written in Hebrew characters].
> Typescript pp. 24.
> *Classed inventory*. Includes descriptions of the Hebrew items acquired since
> 1936.

## For the Gaster collection, see:

*Hebrew and Samaritan manuscripts of the Gaster Collection in the British
Museum*. Photocopy of a handwritten list. pp. 203.
> *Conversion tables: Or.-Gaster; Gaster-Or.* Typescript.

## For Judaeo-Persian items, see:

ROSENWASSER, J. *Judaeo-Persian manuscripts in the British Museum*. London
1968. Offprint from *Handlist of Persian manuscripts* 1895–1966 [by G. M.
Meredith-Owens].
> Describes 69 Judaeo-Persian items, bound as 45 volumes. With indexes of
> persons and of titles.

**See also:**

HOERNING, R. *Description and collation of six Karaite manuscripts of portions of the Hebrew Bible in Arabic characters.* London 1889. pp. xii, 69; pl. 37. Facsimiles, with transcriptions and annotations.

ABRAHAMS, I. and STOKES, H. P. *Starrs and Jewish charters preserved in the British Museum.* With additions by H. Loewe. Cambridge 1930–32. 3 vols. Texts with translation.

*Digest of commentaries on the tractates Bābhā kammā, Bābhā meṣī'ā and Bābhā bhāthērā of the Babylonian Talmud compiled by Zachariah ben Judah Aghmātī.* Reproduced in facsimile from the unique manuscript in the British Museum Or. 10013. Edited with an introduction by Jacob Leveen. Published by the Trustees of the British Museum. London 1961. pp. xviii, 315.

*The Golden Haggadah.* Facsimile of BM Add. MS. 27210. Published by the Trustees of the British Museum in association with Eugrammia Press Ltd. London 1970. pp. 200.

**For printed books, see:**

ZEDNER, J. *Catalogue of the Hebrew printed books in the Library of the British Museum.* London 1867. Reprinted 1964. pp. 899.
Describes about 10,000 items.

VAN STRAALEN, S. *Catalogue of Hebrew books in the British Museum acquired during the years 1868–1892.* London 1894. pp. 539.
The index of titles also incorporates the titles from the 1867 catalogue.

*Blue-slip catalogue of Hebrew books acquired during the years 1893–1954.*
About 10,000 items.

*Card catalogue of Hebrew books acquired since 1954.*

*Alphabetical and numerical lists of Hebrew periodicals.* Handwritten.

## KARSHUNI

*MSS. 108 ; a few printed books.*
As well as religious works—biblical, liturgical, theological, hagiographical, etc.—there are a few secular works on philosophy, ethics, logic, philology, history and geography, medicine and science, the occult, etc.

**For manuscripts, see:**

ROSEN, F. A. and FORSHALL, J. *Catalogus codicum manuscriptorum orientalium qui in Museo Britannico asservantur. Pars prima, codices Syriacos et Carshunicos amplectens.* London 1838. pp. 152.
Describes 11 Karshuni items on pp. 98–113; index on pp. 115–140.

WRIGHT, W. *Catalogue of Syriac manuscripts in the British Museum, acquired since the year 1838.* 3 vols. London 1870–72. Includes 5 Karshuni items.

MARGOLIOUTH, G. *Descriptive list of Syriac and Karshuni manuscripts in the British Museum acquired since 1873.* London 1899. pp. 64.
Describes 58 Karshuni items, interspersed with the Syriac items. With an index of names and titles.

*Classed inventory.* Includes most of the above and in addition 34 items acquired since 1900.

For printed books, no separate record has been kept, but some Karshuni
items are included in the catalogues of Arabic printed books.

## KURDISH
*MSS. 4 ; PB 130.*
**For manuscripts, see:**
*Kurdish manuscripts in the British Library.* Typescript by P. Waley. 1973. p. 1.
**For printed books, see:**
*Card catalogue of Kurdish books.*

## MALTESE
*PB 700.*
Maltese books are at present normally acquired by the Department of
Printed Books.
**See:**
*Blue-slip catalogue of Maltese books.*
About 350 items in this Department, the majority of them nineteenth century
imprints.

## MANDAIC
*MSS. 18 ; PB about 25.*
The manuscripts comprise 9 complete codices, all liturgical, and 2 volumes
containing 9 fragments of liturgical codices and magical prayer rolls respec-
tively. In addition, the Department of Western Asiatic Antiquities of the
British Museum has a lead prayer-roll.
    The British Library has a comprehensive collection of printed texts,
grammars, etc., about three quarters of which are in the Department of
Printed Books.
**For manuscripts, see:**
WRIGHT, W. *Catalogue of Syriāc manuscripts in the British Museum, acquired
    since the year 1838.* London, 1870–72. 3 vols.
    Appendix B describes 5 codices and 8 fragments.
*Classed inventory.*
**For printed books, see:**
*Card catalogue of Mandaic books.*

## NEO-SYRIAC
*MSS. 15 ; PB about 50.*
**For manuscripts, see:**
MARGOLIOUTH, G. *Descriptive list of Syriac and Karshuni manuscripts in the
    British Museum acquired since 1873.* London 1899. pp. 64.
    Includes 5 Neo-Syriac items. The introduction draws attention to 2 of
    these as being in 'modern Syriac'.
*Classed inventory.* Includes a further 10 Neo-Syriac items acquired since 1900.
**For printed books, see:**
MOSS, C. *Catalogue of Syriac printed books and related literature in the British
    Museum.* London 1962. pp. 8; cols. 1652.
    The introduction points out that 'modern Syriac, which is really a different

language', was included, but that no attempt was made to separate such items.
*Card catalogue of Neo-Syriac printed books acquired since about 1959.*

## NUBIAN
*MSS. 1.*
Of the four literary texts known to date in the language of Christian Nubia in the sixth to twelfth centuries, the only two complete ones are in Or. 6805, which was brought from Edfu by R. de Rustafjaell.
**See:**
DE RUSTAFJAELL, R. *The light of Egypt.* London 1909. pp. 141–9 and pls. 49–51.
BUDGE, E. A. W., ed. *Texts relating to Saint Mena of Egypt and Canons of Nicea in a Nubian dialect.* London 1909. pp. 82; pl. 36. Facsimile edition.
GRIFFITH, F. Ll. The Nubian texts of the Christian period. In: *Abhandlungen der Königlich preussischen Akademie der Wissenschaften,* Jhg. 1913, phil.-hist. Kl. Nr. 8. pp. 134; pl. 3.
ZYHLARZ, E. Grundzüge der nubischen Grammatik im christlicher Frühmittelalter (altnubisch). In: *Abhandlungen für die Kunde des Morgenlandes,* XVIII Bd., Nr. 1. Leipzig 1928. pp. 208.
Printed texts and grammars in modern Nubian dialects are held both in this Department and in the Department of Printed Books. Meroitic is covered by the Department of Egyptian Antiquities of the British Museum and by the Department of Printed Books.

## PASHTO
*MSS. 69 ; PB 525.*
**For manuscripts, see:**
BLUMHARDT, J. F. *Catalogue of Pushtu and Sindhi manuscripts.* pp. 50. In: *Catalogue of the Marathi, Gujarati, Bengali, Assamese, Oriya, Pushtu, and Sindhi manuscripts in the Library of the British Museum.* London 1905. pp. xii, 48, 45, 34, 50.
  Describes 62 Pashto items. Has now been superseded by the following:
BLUMHARDT, J. F. *Catalogue of Pushtu books.* Cols. 54. In: *Catalogue of the in the libraries of the British Isles.* London 1965. pp. 169.
  Includes descriptions of the 69 items in the British Library, based on the Blumhardt catalogue of 1905.
**For printed books, see:**
BLUMHARDT, J. F. *Catalogue of Pushtu books.* Cols. 54. In: *Catalogue of the Hindi, Panjabi, Sindhi and Pushtu printed books in the Library of the British Museum.* London 1893. Cols. 278, 64, 24, 54.
  Describes 200 Pashto items. With indexes of titles and of subjects.
*Card catalogue of Pashto books.* 325 entries.

## PERSIAN
*MSS. 3000 ; PB 10,000, including items in Tajik.*
The quality and extent of the manuscript collection is due largely to the acquisition during the nineteenth century of a number of remarkable private collections, such as those of Rich, Malcolm, Yule, Erskine, Elliot and

**4 Persian.** Majnūn is brought to the tent of Lailā. Painted by Mīr Sayyīd 'Alī for a
MS. of the Khamsa of Niẓāmī prepared for Shāh Ṭahmāsp. Tabriz, 1539–43.
Or. 2265, f. 157b.

Hamilton. The illustrated manuscripts contain some of the finest examples of the various styles of painting and illumination, and are complemented by the individual paintings and album leaves in the Department of Oriental Antiquities in the British Museum.

**For manuscripts, see:**

RIEU, C. *Catalogue of the Persian manuscripts in the British Museum*. London 1879–1883. 3 vols. Reprinted 1966.

> Describes 2536 items, arranged by subject. With indexes of titles and of persons' names.

RIEU, C. *Supplement to the catalogue of the Persian manuscripts in the British Museum*. London 1895. pp. 317.

> Describes 425 items.

MEREDITH-OWENS, G. M. *Handlist of Persian manuscripts acquired by the British Museum from 1895–1966*. London 1968. pp. 136.

> Brief descriptions of 973 manuscripts, including 69 Judaeo-Persian items described in a separate section by J. Rosenwasser. With indexes of personal names and of titles.

*Blue-slip catalogue of Persian manuscripts acquired since 1966.*

*Classed inventory.*

**See also:**

EDWARDS, E., ed. *Facsimile of the manuscript of Dīwāni Zu'l Faḳar*. London 1934. pp. 474. A facsimile of Or. 9777.

**For miniatures and illustrated manuscripts, see:**

MEREDITH-OWENS, G. M. *Persian illustrated manuscripts*. London 1965. Revised edition 1973. pp. 32; pl. 24.

> A general introduction to Persian miniature painting, with special reference to the Department's collection.

TITLEY, N. M. *Persian Illustrated Manuscripts : Catalogue and subject index of miniatures from Persian manuscripts and albums in the British Library and the British Museum*. London 1977. pp. 377; pl. 41.

> Describes about 11,000 miniatures, covering a wide variety of styles of painting, from illustrated Persian manuscripts in the Department's collection. Also includes over 800 single Persian and Mughal miniatures and album leaves in the Department of Oriental Antiquities of the British Museum. With an extensive subject index covering each individual miniature, as well as indexes of authors, titles, artists and styles.

**For printed books, see:**

EDWARDS, E. *Catalogue of the Persian printed books in the British Museum*. London 1922. pp. viii; cols. 968.

> Describes about 4000 items. With indexes of titles and of subjects. The first detailed catalogue of any large collection of Persian printed books.

*Card catalogue of Persian printed books acquired since 1922.* About 5500 items.

## SAMARITAN

*MSS. 148.*

**For manuscripts, see:**

MARGOLIOUTH, G., ed. *Descriptive list of Hebrew and Samaritan manuscripts in the British Museum*. London 1893. pp. 138. 63 Samaritan items are described on pp. 89–94.

*Hebrew and Samaritan manuscripts of the Gaster collection in the British Museum.* Photostat copy of a handwritten list. Including brief descriptions of 68 Samaritan items.

*Classed inventory:* Includes a further 17 Samaritan items.

Some printed editions of Samaritan texts are incorporated in the catalogues of Hebrew printed books.

## SWAHILI
*MSS. 11.*

The manuscripts are in Arabic script. Swahili printed books are held in the Department of Printed Books.

**See:**

*Classed inventory.*

## SYRIAC
*MSS. 1160 volumes, comprising over 1500 works; PB about 1000. These include Karshuni and Christian Aramaic, but not Mandaic.*

Claudius Rich collected 66 volumes at Mosul, purchased by the Museum in 1825. During the next forty years, nearly 600 more volumes were acquired mostly from monasteries of the Wadi Natrun; 50 from Urmia and 100 from Mosul had been added by the end of the last century. A further 140 volumes have been acquired since.

**See also:** KARSHUNI and NEO-SYRIAC.

**For manuscripts, see:**

ROSEN, F. A. and FORSHALL, J. *Catalogus codicum manuscriptorum orientalium qui in Museo Britannico asservantur. Pars prima, codices Syriacos et Carshunicos amplectens.* London 1838. pp. 152.

  90 works in 76 volumes on pp. 1–98. Index on pp. 115–40.

WRIGHT, W. *Catalogue of Syriac manuscripts in the British Museum, acquired since the year 1838.* London 1870–72. 3 vols.

  1036 items in 769 volumes.

MARGOLIOUTH, G. *Descriptive list of Syriac and Karshuni manuscripts in the British Museum acquired since 1873.* London 1899. pp. 64.

  250 works in 178 volumes.

*Classed inventory.* Over 100 Syriac items not included above, and, under a separate heading, 34 Karshuni items.

GOTTSTEIN, M. H. A list of some uncatalogued Syriac biblical manuscripts. In: *Bulletin of the John Rylands Library.* Vol. 37 (1954), pp. 429–45.

LEIDEN. The Peshitta Institute. *List of Old Testament Peshitta manuscripts.* 1961. pp. 125.

  British Library Syriac Old Testament manuscripts, pp. 12–26.

**For miniatures, see:**

DE JERPHANION, G., ed. *Les miniatures du manuscrit syriaque No. 559 de la Bibliothèque Vaticane.*

  Miniatures in Or. 7170.

BUCHTHAL, H. and KURZ, O. *Hand list of illuminated oriental Christian manuscripts.* London 1942. pp. 120.

  Includes 27 Syriac items from the Department's collection.

**5 Syriac.** The Nativity, from a Gospel Lectionary from Mar Mattai Monastery. North-east Iraq, 1216–20. Add. 7170, f. 21a.

**For printed books, see:**

Moss, C. *Catalogue of Syriac printed books and related literature in the
British Museum*. London 1962. pp. 8; cols. 1652.
*Card catalogue of Syriac printed books acquired since about 1959.*
Items in Neo-Syriac are now filed separately.

**See also:**

Gaur, A. *Catalogue of Malayalam books in the British Museum*. London 1971.
pp. 27; cols. 588.
Includes Syriac items published by the St Thomas Christians of Kerala.


**TURKISH**

*MSS. 1700 ; PB 6000. These figures include modern Turkish and other languages
of the Turkic group.*

There are a number of Old Turkish documents in runic, Manichaean and
Uygur scripts, some of which were brought from Central Asia by Sir Marc
Aurel Stein. The collection of Islamic Turkish manuscripts includes works
in eastern Turkish and in Azeri as well as in Ottoman. Among its sources
were the Harleian collection, and those of Claudius Rich, Alexandre Jaba,
Col. Hilgrove Turner and Sidney Churchill. The collection includes many
important examples of Ottoman, and some of Persian, miniature painting.

The collection of printed books includes items in modern and Ottoman
Turkish and the Turkic languages of Central Asia. *See* INDEX OF LANGUAGES.

**For manuscripts, see:**

Rieu, C. *Catalogue of the Turkish manuscripts in the British Museum*. London
1888. pp. 371.
Describes 483 items, including 39 in Eastern Turkish and 8 in Azeri. With
lists of pre-1483 and illuminated manuscripts, and indexes of titles,
persons' names, and subjects.
*Temporary handlist of Turkish manuscripts, 1888–1958.* Typescript by
G. M. Meredith-Owens. pp. 48.
About 950 items, arranged by subject. With a separate section for Eastern
Turkish items.
*Blue-slip catalogue of Turkish manuscripts acquired since 1888.* Includes about
300 items acquired since 1958.

**For Old Turkish manuscripts, see:**

*Preliminary list of manuscripts in languages of Central Asia and Sanskrit, from
the collections made by Sir Marc Aurel Stein, K.C.I.E.* Typescript by L. D.
Barnett. pp. 18. 6 Kök Turkish and about 60 Uygur items.

**For miniatures and illustrated manuscripts, see:**

Meredith-Owens, G. M. *Turkish miniatures*. London 1963. Reprinted 1970.
pp. 32; pl. 23.
A brief account of Turkish miniature painting, with special reference to
the Department's collection.
*Handlist of Turkish illustrated manuscripts in the British Museum.* Typescript
by G. M. Meredith-Owens. 1963. pp. 2. Short descriptions of a further 14
manuscripts not described in the above.
*Catalogue and subject index of miniatures from Turkish manuscripts.* In preparation by N. M. Titley.

**For printed books, see:**
*Card catalogue of Turkish books.*
**See also:**
MEREDITH-OWENS, G. M. *The literature of the Turkish peoples.* London 1967.
  Reproduced from typescript.
  A booklet describing the exhibition held in honour of the visit of the
  President of the Turkish Republic in 1967.

## OTHER IRANIAN LANGUAGES
*MSS. 40 ; PB 450.*
In addition to items in PERSIAN, including Tajik, KURDISH and PASHTO (q.v.),
the Department has items in other Iranian languages, of the pre-Islamic and
Islamic periods. *See* INDEX OF LANGUAGES.
**For manuscripts, see:**
*Preliminary list of manuscripts in languages of Central Asia and Sanskrit, from
  the collections made by Sir Marc Aurel Stein, K.C.I.E.* Typescript by L. D.
  Barnett. pp. 18.
  35 Soghdian items, 1 Kuchean and 1 Khotanese item.
*Classed inventory.*
**For printed books, see:**
*Card catalogue of books in Iranian languages.* About 500 items in languages
  other than Persian, Kurdish and Pashto.

# South Asia

## ASSAMESE

*MSS. 15 ; PB 1800.*

**For manuscripts, see:**

BLUMHARDT, J. F. *Catalogue of Bengali, Assamese and Oriya manuscripts.* pp. 34. In: *Catalogue of the Marathi, Gujarati, Bengali, Assamese, Oriya, Pushtu, and Sindhi manuscripts in the Library of the British Museum.* London 1905. pp. xii, 48, 45, 34, 50.

Describes 6 Assamese items. With indexes of titles, persons' names and subjects.

*Classed inventory.* Includes 9 items acquired since 1906.

**For printed books, see:**

[BLUMHARDT, J. F.] *Catalogue of Assamese books.* Cols. 10. In: *Catalogue of Assamese and Oriya books.* London [1900]. Cols. 10, 34.

About 70 items. With an index of titles. No title page; it was probably intended to be incorporated into a larger work.

*Blue-slip catalogue of Assamese books.* About 700 items acquired before about 1945.

*Card catalogue of Assamese books.* About 1000 items acquired subsequently.

**See also:**

*Proscribed Indian books* (temporary list 1968). Xerox typescript. Pages unnumbered. Includes 5 Assamese items. For further details of this catalogue, *see* HINDI.

## BENGALI

*MSS. 32 ; PB 16,000.*

The manuscripts include items from the foundation collections, and other early collections such as those of Halhed and Erskine.

**For manuscripts, see:**

BLUMHARDT, J. F. *Catalogue of Bengali, Assamese, and Oriya manuscripts.* pp. 34. In: *Catalogue of the Marathi, Gujarati, Bengali, Assamese, Oriya, Pushtu and Sindhi manuscripts in the Library of the British Museum.* London 1905. pp. xii, 48, 45, 34, 50.

24 Bengali items. With indexes of titles, persons' names, and subjects.

*Classed inventory.* Includes 8 items acquired since 1906.

CAṬṬOPĀDHYĀY, Sunīti-kumār. Britis Miujiyamer katakguli Baṅgālā Kāghazpatra. In: *Sāhitya-pariṣat patrika'.* Vol. 29 (1923), pp. 109–26. Calcutta.

Bengali documents in manuscript in the Department.

**For printed books, see:**

BLUMHARDT, J. F. *Catalogue of Bengali printed books in the Library of the British Museum.* London 1886. pp. 164.

About 2500 items. With an index of titles.

BLUMHARDT, J. F. *Supplementary catalogue of Bengali books in the Library of*

*the British Museum, acquired during the years 1886–1910.* London 1910.
pp. 7; cols. 470.
About 3000 items. With indexes of titles and of subjects.
BLUMHARDT, J. F. and WILKINSON, J. V. S. *Second supplementary catalogue of
Bengali books in the Library of the British Museum, acquired during the years
1911–1934.* London 1939. pp. 5; cols. 678.
About 5000 items. With indexes of titles and of subjects. Begun by Blum-
hardt, and finished by Wilkinson after Blumhardt's death.
*Blue-slip catalogue of Bengali books acquired 1935–58.* About 3000 items.
*Card catalogue of Bengali books acquired since 1959.* About 2500 items.
**See also:**
*Proscribed Indian books* (temporary list 1968). Xerox typescript. Pages un-
numbered. Includes 95 Bengali items. For further details of this catalogue,
*see* HINDI.

## GUJARATI
*MSS. 71; PB 8100.*
Most of the manuscripts are from the Erskine collection. They include many
important works on Jainism, such as those acquired from the library of
Ratnavijaya Suri of Ahmedabad, and the items collected in the 1870s by
Jacobi.
**For manuscripts, see:**
BLUMHARDT, J. F. *Catalogue of Gujarati manuscripts.* pp. 45. In: *Catalogue of
the Marathi, Gujarati, Bengali, Assamese, Oriya, Pushtu, and Sindhi manu-
scripts in the Library of the British Museum.* London 1905. pp. xii, 48, 45,
34, 50.
57 Gujarati items, including some Gujarati glosses on Jain texts in Prakrit
and Sanskrit. With indexes of titles, subjects, and persons' names.
*Classed inventory.* Includes 14 Gujarati items acquired since 1906.
**See also:**
GAUR, A. *Indian Charters on Copper Plates.* London 1975. pp. 53; pl. 12.
Includes 2 Gujarati items. For further details of this catalogue, *see* SAN-
SKRIT and PRAKRIT.
**For printed books, see:**
BLUMHARDT, J. F. *Catalogue of Gujarati books.* Cols. 196. In: *Catalogue of
Marathi and Gujarati printed books in the Library of the British Museum.*
London 1892. Cols. 232, 196.
About 2700 Gujarati items. With indexes of titles and of subjects.
BLUMHARDT, J. F. *Supplementary catalogue of Gujarati printed books.* Cols.
336. In: *Supplementary catalogue of Marathi and Gujarati printed books in
the British Museum.* London 1915. Cols. 256, 336.
About 2000 Gujarati items. With indexes of titles and of subjects.
*Blue-slip catalogue of Gujarati books acquired 1916–56.* About 2000 items.
*Card catalogue of Gujarati books acquired since 1957.* 1400 items.
**See also:**
*Proscribed Indian books* (temporary list 1968). Xerox typescript. Pages un-

numbered. 49 Gujarati items. For further details of this catalogue, *see* HINDI.

## HINDI

*MSS. 119 ; PB about 18,000.*

Many of the manuscripts are from the Erskine and Hamilton collections, and include works of medieval religious poetry, concerned particularly with the Rāma and Kṛṣṇa cults.

### For manuscripts, see:

BLUMHARDT, J. F. *Catalogue of Hindi and Panjabi manuscripts.* pp. 84. In: *Catalogue of the Hindi, Panjabi and Hindustani manuscripts in the Library of the British Museum.* London 1899. pp. xii, 84, 91.
Describes 93 Hindi items. With indexes of titles, persons' names and subjects.

*Handlist of Hindi manuscripts acquired since 1900.* Typescript by G. W. Shaw. 1974. pp. 5. Describes 26 items.

### See also:

GAUR, A. *Indian Charters on Copper Plates.* London 1975. pp. 53; pl. 12.
Includes 1 item in Rajasthani dialect. For further details of this catalogue, *see* SANSKRIT and PRAKRIT.

### For printed books, see:

BLUMHARDT, J. F. *Catalogue of Hindi books.* Cols. 278. In: *Catalogue of the Hindi, Panjabi, Sindhi, and Pushtu printed books in the Library of the British Museum.* London 1893. Cols. 278, 64, 24, 54.
About 2500 items. With indexes of titles and of subjects.

BLUMHARDT, J. F. *Supplementary catalogue of Hindi books in the Library of the British Museum acquired during the years 1893–1912.* London 1913. pp. 2; cols. 470.
About 3300 items. Some non-Hindi items in Devanagari script are incorporated.

BARNETT, L. D., BLUMHARDT, J. F. and WILKINSON, J. V. S. *Second supplementary catalogue of printed books in Hindi, Bihari (including Bhojpuria, Kaurmali and Maithili), and Pahari (including Nepali or Khaskura, Jaunsari, Mandeali, etc.) in the Library of the British Museum.* London 1957. pp. viii; cols. 1678.
6444 items. With indexes of titles and of subjects, and indexes of titles of non-Hindi books, classified by language.

*Card catalogue of Hindi books acquired since 1956.* About 5700 items.

### For proscribed books, see:

*Proscribed Indian books* (temporary list 1968). Xerox typescript. Pages unnumbered.
A title list of some 1200 books and pamphlets proscribed under the Indian Press Act of 1910 and deposited in the British Museum between 1915 and 1947. Much of the material relates to the campaign for independence launched by the Congress Party from the 1920s onwards. Being withdrawn from circulation, the material was viewable only with permission of the Secretary of State for India; but since 1968, the collection has been open

to public inspection. It is only now in the process of being fully catalogued
on cards, and the following list is therefore only approximate. The languages represented are: Assamese (5), Bengali (95), Burmese (2), Gujarati
(49), Hindi (536, in Devanagari and Arabic scripts), Kannada (10),
Malayalam (2), Marathi (65), Oriya (7), Panjabi (51), Sindhi (21), Tamil
(26), Telugu (15), Urdu (168), English (75), English and vernacular (4).

BARRIER, N. G. South Asia in vernacular publications: modern Indian
    language collections in the British Museum and the India Office Library,
    London. In: *Journal of Asian Studies*. Vol. 28, No. 4 (1969), pp. 803–10.

BARRIER, N. G. *Banned : controversial literature and political control in British
    India 1907–1947*. Columbia 1974.

    Based on material in the British Library, the India Office Library, and the
    National Archives, Delhi. Includes information on the banned publica-
    tions in Hindi, Panjabi and Urdu in the Department, with references to
    the shelf marks.

## KANNADA
*MSS. 40 ; PB 10,000.*
**For manuscripts, see:**
*Handlist of Dravidian manuscripts in the British Library*. In preparation by
    A. Gaur. For further details of this catalogue, *see* TAMIL.
GAUR, A. *Indian Charters on Copper Plates*. London 1975. pp. 53; pl. 12.
    Includes 16 Kannada items. For further details of this catalogue, *see*
    SANSKRIT and PRAKRIT.
*Classed inventory.*

**6 Sanskrit, Old Kannada.** Copper-plate charter. South India, AD 829. Ind. Ch. 65.

**For printed books, see:**

BARNETT, L. D. *Catalogue of the Kannada, Badaga and Kurg books in the Library of the British Museum.* London 1910. pp. 5; cols. 278.
   About 2800 items. With indexes of titles and of subjects.

*Blue-slip catalogue of books in Kannada and related languages acquired 1911–64.* About 6000 items.

*Card catalogue of Kannada books acquired since 1965.* About 1200 items.

**See also:**

*Proscribed Indian books* (temporary list 1968). Xerox typescript. Pages unnumbered. Includes 10 Kannada items. For further details of this catalogue, *see* HINDI.


## KASHMIRI

*MSS. 6; PB 132.*

**For manuscripts, see:**

*Classed inventory.*

**For printed books, see:**

*Blue-slip catalogue of Kashmiri books acquired before 1966.* 120 items.

*Card catalogue of Kashmiri books acquired since 1967.* 12 items.


## MALAYALAM

*MSS. 40; PB 7000.*

The collection of printed books is comprehensive. Early publications not available elsewhere include one dated 1772, the first book published in Malayalam characters, and lithographs in modified Arabic characters published by the Māppiḷa community of Kerala.

**For manuscripts, see:**

*Handlist of Dravidian manuscripts in the British Library.* In preparation by A. Gaur. For further details of this catalogue, *see* TAMIL.

*Classed inventory.*

**For printed books, see:**

GAUR, A. *Catalogue of Malayalam books in the British Museum.* London 1971. pp. 27; cols. 588.
   The first published catalogue of Malayalam printed books. Describes about 5000 items. With an appendix listing the books in Brahui, Gondi, Kui, Malto, Oraon (Kurukh), Toda and Tulu. The introduction includes a short history of Malayalam literature. With indexes of authors, titles and subjects.

*Card catalogue of Malayalam books acquired since 1971.* 1600 items.

**See also:**

*Proscribed Indian books* (temporary list 1968). Xerox typescript. Pages unnumbered. Includes 2 Malayalam items. For further details of this catalogue, *see* HINDI.


## MANIPURI

*MSS. 3; PB 150.*

**For manuscripts, see:**

*Classed inventory.*

**For printed books, see:**

*Card catalogue of Manipuri books.*

## MARATHI
*MSS. 79; PB 8000.*
Most of the manuscripts are from the collections of William Erskine and the Revd Benjamin Webb; they include several important works on the history of medieval Maharashtra and Rajputana.
**For manuscripts, see:**
BLUMHARDT, J. F. *Catalogue of Marathi manuscripts.* pp. 48. In: *Catalogue of the Marathi, Gujarati, Bengali, Assamese, Oriya, Pushtu, and Sindhi manuscripts in the Library of the British Museum.* London 1905. pp. xii, 48, 45, 34, 50.
  Describes 74 Marathi items. With indexes of titles, persons' names, and subjects.
*Classed inventory.* Describes the 5 items acquired since 1906.
**For printed books, see:**
BLUMHARDT, J. F. *Catalogue of Marathi books.* Cols. 232. In: *Catalogue of Marathi and Gujarati printed books in the Library of the British Museum.* London 1892. Cols. 232, 196.
  Describes about 1700 items. With indexes of titles and of subjects. This is believed to be the first library catalogue ever made of Marathi books.
BLUMHARDT, J. F. *Supplementary catalogue of Marathi printed books.* Cols. 256. In: *Supplementary catalogue of Marathi and Gujarati printed books in the British Museum.* London 1915. Cols. 256, 336.
  Describes about 1500 items. With indexes of titles and of subjects.
*Blue-slip catalogue of Marathi books acquired 1916–1942.* 2500 items.
*Card catalogue of Marathi books acquired since 1943.* 2300 items.
**See also:**
*Proscribed Indian books* (temporary list 1968). Xerox typescript. Pages unnumbered. Includes 65 Marathi items. For further details, *see* HINDI.

## NEPALI
*MSS. 15; PB 420.*
The manuscripts include several Nepali versions of Sanskrit works, Buddhist texts, and a petition from an early nineteenth century Maharaja of Nepal to the Emperor of China.
**For manuscripts, see:**
BLUMHARDT, J. F. *Catalogue of Hindi and Panjabi manuscripts.* pp. 84. In: *Catalogue of the Hindi, Panjabi and Hindustani manuscripts in the Library of the British Museum.* London 1899. pp. xii, 84, 91.
  Item 1 is in fact a Roman Missal 'translated into the Parbatiya, or Nepali, dialect of Hindi'.
*Handlist of manuscripts in Nepali, Newari and Sanskrit.* Typescript by G. E. Marrison. 1973. pp. 5. Describes about 60 items from Nepal, including the 15 wholly or partly in Nepali.
**For printed books, see:**
BARNETT, L. D., BLUMHARDT, J. F. and WILKINSON, J. V. S. *Second supplementary catalogue of printed books in Hindi, Bihari (including Bhojpuria, Kaurmali and Maithili), and Pahari (including Nepali or Khaskura, Jaunsari, Mandeali, etc.) in the Library of the British Museum.* London 1957. pp. viii; cols. 1678. Includes about 220 Nepali items.
*Card catalogue of Nepali books acquired since 1958.* About 200 items.

## NEWARI
*MSS. 8 ; PB 100.*
**For manuscripts, see:**
*Handlist of manuscripts in Nepali, Newari and Sanskrit.* Typescript by G. E.
  Marrison. 1973. pp. 5. Describes about 60 items from Nepal, including the
  8 wholly or partly in Newari.
**For printed books, see:**
*Card catalogue of Newari books.* About 100 items.

## ORIYA
*MSS. 25 ; PB 2400.*
20 of the manuscripts are on palm-leaves, the rest on paper.
**For manuscripts, see:**
BLUMHARDT, J. F. *Catalogue of Bengali, Assamese, and Oriya manuscripts.*
  pp. 34. In: *Catalogue of the Marathi, Gujarati, Bengali, Assamese, Oriya,
  Pushtu, and Sindhi manuscripts in the Library of the British Museum.*
  London 1905. pp. xii, 48, 45, 34, 50.
  Describes 12 Oriya items. With indexes of titles, persons' names, and
  subjects.
*Classed inventory.* Lists the 13 items acquired since 1906.
**For printed books, see.**
[BLUMHARDT, J. F.] *Catalogue of Oriya books.* Cols. 34. In: *Catalogue of As-
  samese and Oriya books.* London [1900]. Cols. 10, 34.
  About 200 items. With index of titles. Although this catalogue has no title
  page, it is undoubtedly by Blumhardt, and was probably intended to be
  subsequently incorporated into a larger work.
*Blue-slip catalogue of Oriya books acquired 1900–57.* About 1500 items.
*Card catalogue of Oriya books acquired since 1958.* About 700 items.
**See also:**
*Proscribed Indian books* (temporary list 1968). Xerox typescript. Pages un-
  numbered. Includes 7 Oriya items. For further details of this catalogue, *see*
  HINDI.

## PALI
*MSS. about 1100 ; PB about 2000.*
The Pali manuscripts derive both from Ceylon and South East Asia, chiefly
Burma, but with some from Cambodia, Laos and Thailand. The Nevill
collection from Ceylon includes some 1500 Pali items in 450 *pot*, many with
Sinhalese translations or commentaries.
    The printed books were acquired largely through copyright legislation in
force in Ceylon and Burma.
**For manuscripts, see:**
*Catalogue of mainland South East Asia manuscripts in the British Library.* In
  preparation by P. M. Herbert, G. E. Marrison and H. Ginsburg. Will
  include descriptions of all the South East Asian Pali items in the British
  Library.
SOMADASA, K. D. *Laṅkāve puskoḷa pot-nāmāvaliya.* Vol. 3. Colombo 1964.
  pp. 198.
  Lists all the Pali manuscripts in the British Library. For further details of

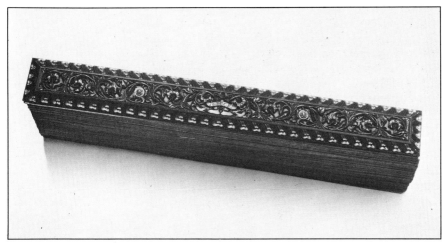

**7 Pali.** Palm-leaf. Manuscript of Buddhaghosa's Visuddhimagga, with carved ebony covers. Ceylon, nineteenth century. Or. 2246.

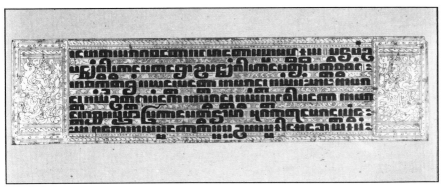

**8 Pali.** Felt made from cast-off royal robes, stiffened and gilt. From a Kammavācā in Burmese square script. Burma, nineteenth century. Or. 12891, f. 1b.

this catalogue, *see* SINHALESE.

*List of Sinhalese and Pali manuscripts in the British Library.* Typescript by J. Hettiaracchi 1974. A translation of the above.

HOERNING, K. J. R. List of [Pali] manuscripts in the British Museum. In *Journal of the Pali Text Society 1883.* pp. 133–44. London. A classed list of about 110 items.

HOERNING, K. J. R. List of Pali manuscripts in the British Museum, acquired since 1883. Prepared as a supplement to the list published in the *Journal of the Pali Text Society* for that year. In: *Journal of the Pali Text Society 1888.* pp. 108–11. London. A classed list of 64 items.

*Descriptive list of Pali manuscripts.* In manuscript by R. Hoerning. 1889. With further additions up to 1903. ff. 96. Describes about 300 manuscripts. With a classified index.

*List of Pali manuscripts, excluding the Nevill collection.* Typescript by L. D.

Barnett. 1930. pp. 70. A revised version of the above list. With index of titles.

*Classed inventory.* Includes the few Pali items acquired since 1931.

**For Pali items in the Nevill collection, see also:**

*Catalogue of the Nevill collection ( prose).* In manuscript by H. Nevill. 4 vols. Includes brief descriptions of a small number of the Pali items in the Nevill collection. Vol. 4 comprises an index of the Kathavastu literature and a description of Pali literature in Ceylon.

*List of Pali, Sinhalese, Sanskrit and other manuscripts, formerly in the possession of Hugh Nevill Esq.* In manuscript by L. D. Barnett. 1909. 2 vols. Includes brief descriptions of about 450 Pali manuscripts.

For further details of the above catalogues of the Nevill collection, *see* SINHALESE.

**For printed books, see:**

HAAS, E. *Catalogue of Sanskrit and Pali books in the British Museum.* London 1876. pp. 196.

Includes about 50 Pali items. With index of titles.

BENDALL, C. *Catalogue of Sanskrit, Pali and Prakrit books in the British Museum acquired during the years 1876–1892.* London 1893. pp. 10; cols. 624. Includes about 250 Pali items. With indexes of titles and of subjects.

BARNETT, L. D. *Supplementary catalogue of Sanskrit, Pali and Prakrit books in the Library of the British Museum acquired during the years 1892–1906.* London 1908. pp. 8; cols. 1096.

Includes about 300 Pali items. With indexes of titles and of subjects.

BARNETT, L. D. *Supplementary catalogue of the Sanskrit, Pali and Prakrit books in the Library of the British Museum acquired during the years 1906–1928.* London 1928. pp. 9; cols. 1694.

Includes 500 Pali items. With indexes of titles and of subjects.

*Blue-slip catalogue of Sanskrit, Pali and Prakrit books acquired 1926–70.* Includes about 700 Pali items. With a title index. Is in the process of being incorporated into the following:

*Card catalogue of Sanskrit, Pali and Prakrit books acquired since 1928.* Includes about 200 Pali items.

*Fourth supplementary catalogue of the Sanskrit, Pali and Prakrit books in the British Library.* In preparation by J. P. Losty.

Will include all the items acquired since 1928.

## PANJABI

*MSS. 26 ; PB 3625. Both figures include items in Gurmukhi and Arabic scripts.* The manuscripts include items on religion (especially Sikhism), history, biography, poetry, etc., some of them being from the Elliot, Erskine and Fisher collections.

**For manuscripts, see:**

BLUMHARDT, J. F. *Catalogue of Hindi and Panjabi manuscripts.* pp. 84. In: *Catalogue of the Hindi, Panjabi and Hindustani manuscripts in the Library of the British Museum.* London 1899. pp. xii, 84, 91.

Describes 14 Panjabi items. With indexes of titles, persons' names and subjects.

*Classed inventory.* Includes 12 items acquired since 1899.

**For printed books, see:**

BLUMHARDT, J. F. *Catalogue of Panjabi books.* Cols. 64. In: *Catalogue of the Hindi, Panjabi, Sindhi, and Pushtu printed books in the Library of the British Museum.* London 1893. Cols. 278, 64, 24, 54.

Describes 425 Panjabi items. With indexes of titles and of subjects.

BARNETT, L. D. *Panjabi printed books in the British Museum. A supplementary catalogue.* London 1961. pp. 130.

About 1300 items. With indexes of titles and of subjects.

*Card catalogue of Panjabi books acquired since 1960.* About 1900 items.

**See also:**

*Proscribed Indian books* (temporary list 1968). Xerox typescript. Pages unnumbered. Includes 51 Panjabi items. For further details of this catalogue, *see* HINDI.

## SANSKRIT AND PRAKRIT

*MSS. about 1500 ; PB 25,000.*

The manuscript collection includes a fine group of tenth to fourteenth century palm-leaf manuscripts in Sanskrit from Eastern India, Nepal and elsewhere; some important Buddhist manuscripts of the first millennium AD, on palm-leaf, birch-bark and paper, found in Kashmir and Central Asia; about 350 Jain manuscripts, some 100 of them in Prakrit with Sanskrit commentaries, most of which were collected by Jacobi in Western Rajasthan and by Ratnavijaya Suri in Ahmedabad. 190 Sanskrit manuscripts were acquired from Erskine and there are 153 in the Nevill collection.

The collection of printed books was formed largely through the copyright legislation in force between 1867 and 1947; it includes the whole range

**9 Sanskrit.** The Buddha from the Aṣṭasāhasrikā Prajñāpāramitā Sūtra. Eastern India, mid-twelfth century. Or. 12461, ff. 123 and 169.

of early Sanskrit imprints from European presses and from the mission presses of India. There are about 1000 Prakrit texts, the majority of which have Sanskrit commentaries.

**For manuscripts, see:**

BENDALL, C. *Catalogue of the Sanskrit manuscripts in the British Museum.* London 1902. pp. 270.
About 600 items. With indexes of titles and of authors, and a general index. Jain items are not included.

*Catalogue of Sanskrit and Prakrit manuscripts in the British Museum.* Vol. II. Typescript by J. P. Losty. 1972. ff. 70.
Lists all the Jain items, which number about 300; and about 500 non-Jain items acquired since 1902.

*Sanskrit and Prakrit manuscripts.* Draft catalogue in manuscript by J. Brough. 1946. pp. 283. Describes 216 of the items listed in the Losty catalogue of 1972, including most of the important Jain ones.

*Classed inventory.* Includes descriptions of all 800 items listed in the Losty catalogue of 1972, as well as about 100 MSS. acquired subsequently.

**For Jain items, see also:**

BLUMHARDT, J. F. *Catalogue of Gujarati manuscripts.* pp. 45. In: *Catalogue of the Marathi, Gujarati, Bengali, Assamese, Oriya, Pushtu, and Sindhi manuscripts in the Library of the British Museum.* London 1905. pp. xii, 48, 45, 34, 50.
Includes 25 Jain items in Sanskrit or Prakrit, with Gujarati glosses. With indexes of titles, subjects, and persons' names.

JACOBI, H. Liste der indischen Handschriften im Besitze des Prof. H. Jacobi in Münster i.W. In: *Zeitschrift der Deutschen morgenländischen Gesellschaft.* Bd. 33. Leipzig 1879. pp. 693–7.
Lists 147 Sanskrit and Prakrit items collected by Jacobi in Western Rajasthan.

LEUMANN, E. Liste von transcribierten Abschriften und Auszügen aus der Jaina-Litteratur. In: *Zeitschrift der Deutschen morgenländischen Gesellschaft.* Bd. 47. Leipzig 1893. pp. 308–15.
Based on manuscript material in the libraries of Cambridge and London, including items from the Erskine and Ratnavijaya Suri collections in the British Library.

*Jain manuscripts: temporary list.* Typescript by G. E. Marrison. 1969. pp. 10.
Lists about 300 items in Sanskrit and Prakrit, as well as a few in Hindi and Gujarati.

**For Sanskrit items from Nepal, see:**

*Handlist of manuscripts in Nepali, Newari and Sanskrit.* Typescript by G. E. Marrison. 1973. pp. 5. Describes about 60 items from Nepal, the majority of which are in Sanskrit.

**For Sanskrit items in the Nevill collection, see:**

*Catalogue of the Nevill collection (prose).* In manuscript by H. Nevill. 4 vols.
Describes only a few of the Sanskrit manuscripts in the Nevill collection.

*List of Pali, Sinhalese, Sanskrit and other manuscripts, formerly in the possession of Hugh Nevill Esq.* In manuscript by L. D. Barnett. 1909. 2 vols.

Includes about 150 Sanskrit items.

SOMADASA, K. D. *Laṅkāve puskoḷa pot-nāmāvaliya*. Vol. 3. Colombo 1964. pp. 198. Lists the Sanskrit items in the Nevill collection.

*List of Sinhalese and Pali manuscripts in the British Library*. Typescript by J. Hettiaracchi. 1974. A translation of the above.

For further details of the above catalogues of the Nevill collection, *see* SINHALESE.

**For Sanskrit items in the Stein collection, see:**

*Preliminary list of manuscripts in languages of Central Asia and Sanskrit, from the collections made by Sir Marc Aurel Stein, K.C.I.E.* Typescript by L. D. Barnett. pp. 18. Includes various Sanskrit documents and fragments, and 1 Prakrit roll. For further details of this catalogue, *see* CHINESE.

**See also:**

GAUR, A. *Indian Charters on Copper Plates*. London 1975. pp. 53; pl. 12. Describes 77 charters referring to revenue-free land grants, from all over India. They are written in a variety of languages and scripts, and cover a period of nearly 2000 years. The languages represented are the following: Sanskrit (51 items), Prakrit (1), Kannada (16), Tamil (4), Telugu (5), Javanese (1), Rajasthani (1), Gujarati (2).

**For printed books, see:**

HAAS, E. *Catalogue of Sanskrit and Pali books in the British Museum*. London 1876. pp. 196. About 2000 items. With index of titles.

BENDALL, C. *Catalogue of Sanskrit, Pali and Prakrit books in the British Museum acquired during the years 1876–1892*. London 1893. pp. 10; cols. 624. 2750 items. With indexes of titles and of subjects.

BARNETT, L. D. *Supplementary catalogue of Sanskrit, Pali and Prakrit books in the Library of the British Museum acquired during the years 1892–1906*. London 1908. pp. 8; cols. 1096. 4500 items. With indexes of titles and of subjects.

BARNETT, L. D. *Supplementary catalogue of the Sanskrit, Pali and Prakrit books in the Library of the British Museum acquired during the years 1906–1928*. London 1928. pp. 9; cols. 1694. 6500 items. With indexes of titles and of subjects.

*Blue-slip catalogue of Sanskrit, Pali and Prakrit books acquired 1928–70*. 8000 items. With an index of titles. Is in the process of being incorporated into the following:

*Card catalogue of Sanskrit, Pali and Prakrit books acquired since 1928*. Includes about 3000 items acquired since 1971.

*Fourth supplementary catalogue of the Sanskrit, Pali and Prakrit books in the British Library*. In preparation by J. P. Losty. Will include all the items acquired since 1928.

# SAURĀṢṬRA

*PB 19.*

BARNETT, L. D. *Catalogue of Saurāshtra books in the Library of the British Museum*. London 1960. pp. 12.

19 items, in the Devanagari, Tamil, Telugu and 'Saurāshtran' scripts. Believed to be the first catalogue of books in Saurāstra, a language of the Central group of the Indo-Aryan family, now spoken by a community in Madras.

## SINDHI
*MSS. 32; PB about 1600.*
The manuscripts include items from the Baumgartner and Erskine collections. Many deal with the doctrine and early history of Islam.
**For manuscripts, see:**
BLUMHARDT, J. F. *Catalogue of Pushtu and Sindhi manuscripts.* pp. 50. In: *Catalogue of the Marathi, Gujarati, Bengali, Assamese, Oriya, Pushtu, and Sindhi manuscripts in the Library of the British Museum.* London 1905. pp. xii, 48, 45, 34, 50.
Describes 32 Sindhi items. With indexes of titles, persons' names and subjects.
**For printed books, see:**
BLUMHARDT, J. F. *Catalogue of Sindhi books.* Cols. 24. In: *Catalogue of the Hindi, Panjabi, Sindhi and Pushtu printed books in the Library of the British Museum.* London 1893. pp. 20; cols. 278, 64, 24, 54.
About 150 items. With indexes of titles and of subjects.
*Blue-slip catalogue of Sindhi books acquired 1894–1960.* 1050 items.
*Card catalogue of Sindhi books acquired since 1961.* About 400 items.
**See also:**
*Proscribed Indian books* (temporary list 1968). Xerox typscript. Pages unnumbered. Includes 21 Sindhi items. For further details of this catalogue, *see* HINDI.

## SINHALESE
*MSS. 2500; PB 8000.*
Of the 2227 manuscripts collected in Ceylon by Hugh Nevill, the vast majority are in Sinhalese; this collection was acquired by the Department in 1904, and is the most important such collection outside Ceylon, covering as it does the whole range of Ceylonese literature.
Up to the independence of Ceylon (now Sri Lanka), printed books were acquired under colonial copyright; the relevant act was never repealed in Ceylon and the British Library still receives books by copyright deposit.
**For manuscripts, see:**
WICKREMASINGHE, M. de Z. *Catalogue of the Sinhalese manuscripts in the British Museum.* London 1900. pp. 224.
Describes 140 inscribed *pot.* With indexes of titles, proper names, and subjects.
SOMADASA, K. D. *Laṅkāve puskoḷa pot-nāmāvaliya.* Colombo 1959–64. 3 vols.
A union catalogue of Ceylonese palm-leaf manuscripts in Ceylon and in the British Library. Vols. 1–2 list items in Ceylon. Vol. 3 includes a complete list of all the items in the Nevill collection as well as all the other British Library manuscripts in Pali. The following languages are represented:

Sinhalese (2739 items); Pali in Sinhalese script (about 1550 items, of which
more than half have Sinhalese translation or commentary); Pali in Burmese
script (about 350 items); Sanskrit in Sinhalese script (about 240 items);
Tamil (about 50 items); Telugu (about 25 items); English (about 20 items);
Latin (8 items).

*List of Sinhalese and Pali manuscripts in the British Library.* Typescript by
J. Hettiaracchi. 1974. A translation of Vol. 3 of the above work.

**For the Nevill collection, see also:**

*Catalogue of the Nevill collection.* In manuscript by H. Nevill. 7 vols. Prose
section (in 4 vols.): Vols. 1–3 describe nos. 1–776 in Nevill's numeration,
being items in Sinhalese and Pali. Includes lengthy descriptions, often
with references to comparative material, but without physical descriptions.
Descriptions of Pali items tend to be brief, while many items were never
included. Vol. 4 comprises an index of the Kathāvastu literature and a
description of Pali literature in Ceylon.
Verse section (in 3 vols.): Describes nos. 1–932 in Nevill's numeration,
being the collection of Sinhalese Kavi literature. Similar in style to the
prose section. Each description includes a specimen verse with translation.

NEVILL, H. *Sinhala verse (Kavi). Collected by the late Hugh Nevill, F.Z.S.
(1869–86).* Edited by P. E. P. Deraniyagala. Colombo 1954–55. 3 Vols.
(Ceylon National Museums manuscript series, Vols. 4–6.)
Published from a different draft of the above, found among Nevill's papers
in 1938. Contains nos. 1–911 of the Nevill verse collection. Nos. 1–909
correspond with the Department's draft. Nos. 910–911 are lacking in the
latter, while nos. 912–32 do not appear in this printed version.

*List of Pali, Sinhalese, Sanskrit and other manuscripts, formerly in the pos-
session of Hugh Nevill, Esq.* In manuscript by L. D. Barnett. 1909. Classified by subject, and entered under the British Museum numbers in the
series Or. 6599–6616, with cross-references to Nevill's own catalogue and
numbers. Vol. 3 is a numerical index.

*Handlist of Sinhalese manuscripts.* In manuscript by L. D. Barnett. 1908.
Describes selected items from Or. 6600.

*Conversion tables: Or.—Nevill; Nevill-Or.* Typescript draft. pp. 18, 19. In-
complete.

*Catalogue of the Nevill collection.* Part 1. In preparation by K. D. Somadasa.
Draft available on microfilm.
Brief descriptions, including physical details, of Or. 6599 (1)—Or. 6604
(249), with breakdowns of all the items in any one *pot.*

BARNETT, L. D. *Alphabetical guide to Sinhalese folklore from ballad sources.*
Bombay 1917. pp. 120. Reprinted from *The Indian Antiquary*, supplements
to Vols. 45 and 46, Bombay 1916–17. Most of the headings are proper
names, and the entries are based on the catalogue of the Nevill verse collection. Titles of works are cited, but not the manuscript numbers.

**For printed books, see:**

WICKREMASINGHE, M. de Z. *Catalogue of the Sinhalese printed books in the
Library of the British Museum.* London 1901. pp. 8; cols. 308.
About 2000 items. The compilation was begun by C. Bendall. With indexes

of titles and of subjects.
*Card catalogue of Sinhalese books acquired since 1902.* 6000 items.

## TAMIL
*MSS. 170 ; PB 20,000.*
The manuscripts include two autograph items by Father Beschi and palm-leaf manuscripts written by other European missionaries; they also include items from the Nevill collection.

   The printed books include most of the publications of the Tranquebar Mission Press; these are the oldest surviving Tamil printed books, and go back to 1714.

**For manuscripts, see:**
*Handlist of Dravidian manuscripts in the British Library.* In preparation by
   A. Gaur. Will include all the Dravidian manuscripts in this Department
   and in the Department of (Western) Manuscripts.

**For Tamil items in the Nevill collection, see:**
*Catalogue of the Nevill collection ( prose).* In manuscript by H. Nevill. 4 vols.
   Includes brief descriptions of about 50 Tamil items.
*List of Pali, Sinhalese, Sanskrit and other manuscripts, formerly in the possession
   of Hugh Nevill Esq.* In manuscript by L. D. Barnett. 1909. Includes brief
   descriptions of a few Tanil items.
SOMADASA, K. D. *Laṅkāve puskoḷa pot-nāmāvaliya.* Vol. 3. Colombo 1964. pp.
   198.
   About 50 Tamil items.
*List of Sinhalese and Pali manuscripts in the British Library.* Typescript by
   J. Hettiaracchi. 1974. A translation of the above.

**See also:**
GAUR, A. *Indian Charters on Copper Plates.* London 1975. pp. 53; pl. 12.
   Includes 4 Tamil items. For further details of this catalogue, *see* SANSKRIT
   and PRAKRIT.
*Classed inventory.*
GAUR, A. A catalogue of Ziegenbalg's Tamil Library.  In: *British Museum
   Quarterly,* XXX (1966), pp. 99–105.
   On MS. Sloane 3014.
GAUR, A. Bartholomaeus Ziegenbalg's Verzeichnis der Malabarischen
   Buecher. In: *Journal of the Royal Asiatic Society,* October 1967. pp. 63–95.
   On MS. Sloane 3014.

**For printed books, see:**
BARNETT, L. D. *Catalogue of the Tamil books in the Library of the British
   Museum.* London 1909. pp. 9; cols. 590.
   About 4000 items. With indexes of titles and of subjects. Begun by G. U.
   Pope; revised and continued by L. D. Barnett and A. G. Ellis.
BARNETT, L. D. *Supplementary catalogue of the Tamil books in the Library of
   the British Museum.* London 1931. pp. 8; cols. 696.
   About 6000 items. With indexes of titles and of subjects.
GAUR, A. *Second supplementary catalogue of the Tamil books in the Library of
   the British Museum, 1932–71.* In preparation.

About 8000 items. With indexes of titles and of subjects.
*Card catalogue of Tamil books acquired since 1972.* About 2000 items.
**See also:**
SUBBIAH, R. *Tamil Malaysiana.* Kuala Lumpur 1969. pp. 77.
   Includes a list of all the Tamil books published in Singapore and Malaysia
   in the British Library.
*Proscribed Indian books* (temporary list 1968). Xerox typescript. Pages un-
   numbered. Includes 26 Tamil items. For further details of this catalogue,
   *see* HINDI.

## TELUGU
*MSS. 60 ; PB 12,000.*
Some of the manuscripts are from the Nevill collection.
**For manuscripts, see:**
*Handlist of Dravidian manuscripts in the British Library.* In preparation by
   A. Gaur. For further details of this catalogue, *see* TAMIL.
**For Telugu items in the Nevill collection, see:**
*Catalogue of the Nevill collection (prose).* In manuscript by H. Nevill. 4 vols.
   Includes brief descriptions of 25 Telugu items.
*List of Pali, Sinhalese, Sanskrit and other manuscripts formerly in the pos-
   session of Hugh Nevill Esq.* In manuscript by L. D. Barnett. 1909. Includes
   brief descriptions of 25 Telugu items.
SOMADASA, K. D. *Laṅkāve puskola pot-nāmāvaliya.* Vol. 3. Colombo 1964.
   pp. 198. Lists 25 Telugu items.
   For further details of the above catalogues of the Nevill collection, *see*
   SINHALESE.
**See also:**
GAUR, A. *Indian Charters on Copper Plates.* London 1975. pp. 53; pl. 12.
   5 Telugu items. For further details of this catalogue, *see* SANSKRIT and
   PRAKRIT.
*Classed inventory.*
**For printed books, see:**
BARNETT, L. D. *Catalogue of the Telugu books in the Library of the British
   Museum.* London 1912. pp. 10; cols. 444.
   About 4600 items. With indexes of titles and of subjects.
*Blue-slip catalogue of Telugu books acquired 1912–65.* About 6000 items.
*Card catalogue of Telugu books acquired since 1966.* About 1400 items.
**See also:**
*Proscribed Indian books* (temporary list 1968). Xerox typescript. Pages un-
   numbered. Includes 15 Telugu items. For further details of this catalogue,
   *see* HINDI.

## TIBETAN
*MSS. about 200 ; PB about 3000.*
Of the large collection of Tibetan manuscripts and printed books acquired
by L. A. Waddell during the Younghusband mission of 1904, the greater
part was bought by the British Museum. This includes the manuscript

*Kanjur*, or Tibetan Tripitaka. Further Tibetan items came with the Stein
and Bell collections in 1917 and 1933 respectively. The Department has
items from the seventh century AD onwards and is the most comprehensive
outside Tibet.

Current acquisition of printed books and facsimile editions has been
increasing since about 1955.

**For manuscripts, see:**

*Classed inventory.*

**For the collection made during the Younghusband mission, see:**

WADDELL, L. A. Tibetan manuscripts and books, etc., collected during the
Younghusband Mission to Lhasa. In: *Imperial and quarterly review.* Vol.
34. No. 67. pp. 80–113. Woking 1912.

General description, an account of its distribution between the British
Museum and other libraries, and a list of 464 individual items.

**For the Kanjur manuscript, see:**

BARNETT, L. D. Index der Abteilung mDo des Handschriftlichen *Kanjur* im
Britischen Museum (Or. 6724). In: *Asia Major.* Vol. 7. Fasc. 1/2. pp.
157–78. London 1931.

An annotated table of contents. With an index of Sanskrit titles.

GRINSTEAD, E. D. The manuscript *Kanjur* in the British Museum. In: *Asia
Major.* New series, Vol. 13. Parts 1–2. pp. 1–70. London 1957.

A conversion table from the British Library manuscript to *Complete catalogue of the Tibetan Buddhist Canon,* Tohoku 1934, and *Tibetan Tripitaka,
Peking edition, reprinted,* Otani University, Kyoto 1955–62.

*List of contents of the Tibetan Kanjur in the British Museum (Or. 6724).* Typescript by E. D. Grinstead. Comprises a summary list; a conversion table
to the Otani reprint (q.v. above); a detailed list of contents, with titles in
Sanskrit and Tibetan. Also includes a list of contents of Collection of
Sutras, *mDo-mang,* 19999. b.1.

**For Tibetan items in the Stein collection, see:**

*Preliminary list of manuscripts in languages of Central Asia and Sanskrit, from
the collections made by Sir Marc Aurel Stein, K.C.I.E.* Typescript by L. D.
Barnett. pp. 18. Lists some of the Tibetan documents and fragments from
the Stein collection in the British Library. (Note, however, that the
majority of the Tibetan items in the Stein collection are to be found in the
India Office Library.) For further details of this catalogue, and of the Stein
collection generally, *see* CHINESE.

**For the Bell collection, see:**

*Catalogue of my Tibetan blockprints and manuscripts.* Typescript by Sir
Charles Bell. 1917. Some items from this collection were acquired by the
British Museum in 1933.

**For printed books, see:**

*Blue-slip catalogue of Tibetan printed books.* Over 1000 items, including both
old blockprints and modern editions. In course of revision for incorpora-
tion in:

*Card catalogue of Tibetan printed books.* About 2000 items.

*Catalogue of Tibetan manuscripts, xylographs and printed books in the British Library*. In preparation by Lama Chime Radha. Will describe the entire Tibetan collection.

## URDU
*MSS. 365 ; PB 22,000.*
The manuscripts cover topography, history, religion, biography, poetry, lexicography. Most of them are from the Elliot, Erskine and Hamilton collections. The comprehensive collection of printed books includes many early publications.
**For manuscripts, see:**
BLUMHARDT, J. F. *Catalogue of Hindustani manuscripts.* pp. 91. In : *Catalogue of the Hindi, Panjabi and Hindustani manuscripts in the Library of the British Museum.* London 1899. pp. xii, 84, 91.
 Describes 285 Urdu items. With indexes of titles, persons' names and subjects.
*Temporary handlist of the Urdu manuscripts.* Typescript 1957. pp. 2. Brief descriptions of 31 items acquired since 1897.
*Catalogue of the Urdu manuscripts in the British Library.* In preparation by Q. M. Haq. Will include full descriptions of the 47 items acquired since 1897.
*Classed inventory.*
**For printed books, see:**
BLUMHARDT, J. F. *Catalogue of Hindustani printed books in the Library of the British Museum.* London 1889. pp. 11 ; cols. 458.
 Describes about 3400 items. With indexes of titles and of subjects.
BLUMHARDT, J. F. *Supplementary catalogue of Hindustani books in the Library of the British Museum, acquired during the years 1889–1908.* London 1909. pp. 9 ; cols. 678.
 Describes about 4200 items. With indexes of titles and of subjects.
*Blue-slip catalogue of Urdu books acquired during the years 1910–60.* About 6500 items.
*Second supplementary catalogue of Urdu books in the British Library, acquired during the years 1910–60.* In preparation by Q. M. Haq.
*Card catalogue of Urdu books acquired since 1961.* About 8000 items.
**See also:**
*Proscribed Indian books* (temporary list 1968). Xerox typescript. Pages unnumbered. Includes 168 Urdu items. For further details of this catalogue, *see* HINDI.

## OTHER LANGUAGES OF NORTHERN INDIA
*MSS. 3 ; PB 650.*
In addition to the items in the languages described above, the Department also has 650 books in about 30 other Northern Indian languages of the Indo-Aryan, Dardic, Munda and Tibeto-Burman families. There are separate card and/or blue-slip catalogues for each language. For reference to indi-

vidual languages, *see* INDEX OF LANGUAGES.

**For manuscripts, see:**

BLUMHARDT, J. F. *Catalogue of Bengali, Assamese and Oriya manuscripts.* pp. 34. In: *Catalogue of the Marathi, Gujarati, Bengali, Assamese, Oriya, Pushtu, and Sindhi manuscripts in the Library of the British Museum.* London 1905. pp. xii, 48, 45, 34, 50.

Includes Add. 26594 and Add. 26596, which are vocabularies of Bengali words, with Kuki and Khasi equivalents respectively.

*Classed inventory.* Lists Or. 5383, a legendary account of Sikkim in Lepcha.

**For printed books, see also:**

BARNETT, L. D., BLUMHARDT, J. F. and WILKINSON, J. V. S. *Second supplementary catalogue of printed books in Hindi, Bihari (including Bhojpuria, Kaurmali and Maithili), and Pahari (including Nepali or Khaskura, Jaunsari, Mandeali, etc.) in the Library of the British Museum.* London 1957. pp. viii; cols. 1678.

Besides Hindi and Nepali items, includes about 200 items in other North Indian languages. With indexes of titles and of subjects, and indexes of titles of non-Hindi books, classified by language.

## OTHER DRAVIDIAN LANGUAGES

The Department also has several hundred books in minor Dravidian languages. Card catalogues are available as well as some catalogues published as Appendices to catalogues of major languages. *See* INDEX OF LANGUAGES.

**See also:**

GAUR, A. *Catalogue of Malayalam books in the British Museum.* London 1971. pp. 27; col. 588.

With an appendix listing books in Brahui, Gondi, Kui, Malto, Oraon (Kurukh), Toda and Tulu.

# South East Asia
## with Polynesia and Madagascar

**BALINESE**

*MSS. 9; PB 200.*

The Department is also acquiring typed transcripts of unpublished manuscripts in Balinese and Javanese from Bali through Dr C. Hooykaas. In 1975 these amounted to about 1000 items.

**For manuscripts, see:**

*Indonesian manuscripts in the British Museum.* Typescript by P. Voorhoeve. 1950–54. pp. 15. Brief descriptions of Balinese items are incorporated among the Javanese entries.

*Catalogue of manuscripts in Indonesian languages in the British Museum.* Typescript draft by M. C. Ricklefs and P. Voorhoeve. 1972. pp. 62. Includes fuller descriptions of 8 of the Balinese items.

*Classed inventory.*

HOOYKAAS, C., ed. *Bagus Umbara, Prince of Koripan. The story of a prince of Bali and a princess of Java. Illustrated on palm leaves by a Balinese artist. With Balinese text and English translation.* British Museum, London 1968. pp. 55.

A facsimile of Or. 12579.

**For printed books, see:**

*Card catalogue of Balinese books.* About 200 items.

**BATAK**

*MSS. 15; PB about 75.*

The printed books are in Karo, Toba and Mandailing dialects, and some are in Batak script. They are mostly on educational, linguistic and ethnographical subjects.

**For manuscripts, see:**

*Indonesian manuscripts in the British Museum.* Typescript by P. Voorhoeve. 1950–54. pp. 15.

Includes brief descriptions of 14 of the Batak items.

*Catalogue of manuscripts in Indonesian languages in the British Museum.* Typescript draft by M. C. Ricklefs and P. Voorhoeve. 1972. pp. 62. The draft does not yet include the Batak items, but a Batak section is in preparation.

*Classed inventory.* Includes a description of the Batak item acquired since the compilation of the Voorhoeve list.

**For printed books, see:**

*Card catalogue of Batak books.*

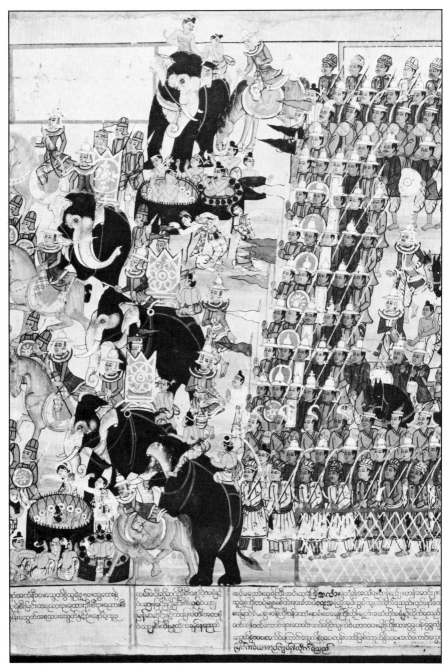

**10 Burmese.** The Procession of King Mindon, from a folding book. Mandalay, nineteenth century. Or. 12013, f. 6.

## BUGIS/MAKASSAR
*MS. 32 ; PB about 80.*
Most of the manuscripts are from the Crawfurd collection.
**For manuscripts, see:**
MATTHES, B. *Kort verslag aangaande alle mij in Europa bekende Makassarsche
en Boegineesche Handschriften.* Amsterdam 1875. pp. 109.
Describes 28 of the Bugis/Makassar manuscripts in the Department on
pp. 89–97.
*Indonesian manuscripts in the British Museum.* Typescript by P. Voorhoeve.
1950–54. pp. 15. Describes 2 Bugis/Makassar items acquired since 1876.
*Catalogue of manuscripts in Indonesian languages in the British Museum.* Type-
script draft by M. C. Ricklefs and P. Voorhoeve. 1972. pp. 62. The draft
does not yet include the Bugis/Makassar items, but a Bugis/Makassar
section is in preparation.
*Classed inventory.* Includes descriptions of the 2 items acquired since 1954.
**For printed books, see:**
*Card catalogue of Bugis/Makassar books.* About 80 items.

## BURMESE
*MSS. about 350, including items in Pali with Burmese glosses (Nissaya);
PB 6000.*
The Burmese manuscript collection is very varied in scope, and is particularly strong in historical, legal and grammatical texts, and in illustrated
material. It includes the John Murray collection, acquired in 1842, in
which there are several manuscripts from Arakan, dating from the 1740s,
and the Sir Arthur Phayre collection, acquired in 1881, of the manuscripts
collected and used by Phayre for his *History of Burma* (London 1883).
Among the items of artistic interest are many folding books (*parabaik*) with
very fine illustrations of court scenes, of the life of the Buddha, and of Jātakas.
**For manuscripts, see:**
PE MAUNG TIN. Burma manuscripts in the British Museum. In: *Journal of
the Burma Research Society.* Vol. 14, part 3 (1924), pp. 221–46. Rangoon.
*List of Pali manuscripts, excluding the Nevill collection.* Typescript by L. D.
Barnett. 1930. pp. 70.
350 Pali manuscripts in Burmese script, some with Burmese glosses or
commentaries.
*Catalogue of mainland South East Asia manuscripts in the British Library.* In
preparation by P. M. Herbert, G. E. Marrison and H. Ginsburg. Will
include full descriptions of all the Burmese items; Pali texts with Burmese
glosses; and Pali manuscripts in Burmese script. This catalogue will
supersede the above two lists.
**See also:**
DUROISELLE, C. Pageant of King Mindon. In: *Memoirs of the Archaeological
Survey of India.* No. 27 (1925). Calcutta, 1925. Contains 15 plates of scenes
from Or. 12013, and descriptive text.
HERBERT, P. M. The Sir Arthur Phayre collection of Burmese manuscripts.
In: *British Library Journal.* Vol. 1, No. 1 (1975), pp. 62–70.

**For printed books, see:**

BARNETT, L. D. *Catalogue of the Burmese books in the British Museum*. London
1913. pp. 353.
    About 2,500 items. Includes Pali texts with Burmese glosses or com-
    mentaries. With indexes of titles and of subjects.
*Blue-slip catalogue of Burmese books acquired 1914–58*. 3000 items. Is in the
    process of being incorporated into:
*Card catalogue of Burmese books*. Includes all the items acquired since 1959.
**See also:**
*Proscribed Indian books* (temporary list 1968). Xerox typescript. Pages un-
    numbered. Includes 2 Burmese items. For further details of this catalogue,
    *see* HINDI.

## CAMBODIAN
*MSS. 8 ; PB 60.*
**For manuscripts, see:**
*Handlist of the Tai and Mon-Khmer manuscripts in the British Museum, to-
    gether with Pali manuscripts from the corresponding region, and a short
    bibliography*. Typescript by G. E. Marrison 1968. pp. 30. Lists the 8
    Cambodian items.
*Catalogue of mainland South East Asia manuscripts in the British Library*.
    In preparation by P. M. Herbert, G. E. Marrison and H. Ginsburg. Full
    descriptions of the 8 Cambodian items.
**For printed books, see:**
*Card catalogue of books in Cambodian.*

## INDONESIAN
*PB 3000.*
Current acquisition is high, and includes the purchase of antiquarian items
from Holland and elsewhere.
**See:**
*Card catalogue of Malay books*. About 1000 Indonesian books acquired before
    1950 are incorporated in this catalogue.
*Card catalogue of Indonesian books acquired since 1951*. About 2000 items.
**For periodicals, see:**
*Periodical publications and newspapers : Malay and Indonesian*. Typescript by
    R. Aboe Hasan. 1970. Describes about 50 Indonesian items.
There are also about 200 Indonesian periodical items in the Official Publica-
tions Library of the British Library.

## JAVANESE
*MSS. 92 ; PB about 1000.*
Many of the manuscripts are from the Crawfurd collection. Besides manuscripts in Modern Javanese, there are also some items in Arabic (Pegon)
script and Kawi items in Old Javanese.
    About 400 of the printed books are in Modern Javanese. There are also
a few text books for Old Javanese, and *Kakawin* in Old Javanese. There are
a few pre-war periodical publications.

**For manuscripts, see:**

RICKLEFS, M. C. An inventory of the Javanese manuscript collection in the British Museum. In: *Bijdragen, Koninklijk Instituut voor Taal-, Land- en Volken-Kunde.* dl. 125. afl. 2. pp. 241–62. The Hague 1969.

*Catalogue of manuscripts in Indonesian languages in the British Museum.* Typescript draft by M. C. Ricklefs and P. Voorhoeve. 1972. pp. 62. 91 Javanese items are described on pp. 4–34.

*Classed inventory.*

**See also:**

GAUR, A. *Indian Charters on Copper Plates.* London 1975. pp. 53; p. 12. Includes 1 Javanese item. For further details of this catalogue, *see* SANSKRIT and PRAKRIT.

**For printed books, see:**

*Card catalogue of Javanese books.* About 1000 items.

## LAO

*MSS. 22; PB 50.*

**For manuscripts, see:**

*Handlist of the Tai and Mon-Khmer manuscripts in the British Museum, together with Pali manuscripts from the corresponding region, and a short bibliography.* Typescript by G. E. Marrison, 1968. pp. 30. Lists 18 Lao items.

*Catalogue of mainland South East Asia manuscripts in the British Library.* In preparation by P. M. Herbert, G. E. Marrison and H. Ginsburg. Full description of all the 22 Lao items.

**For printed books, see:**

*Card catalogue of Lao books.* 50 items.

## MALAY

*MSS. 47; PB about 2000. The Department of (Western) Manuscripts has a further 7 Malay manuscripts. 23 of the manuscripts are from the Crawfurd collection.*

There is extensive coverage of early printed books, including Islamic materials in Jawi script, and a large modern collection.

**For manuscripts, see:**

NIEMANN, G. K. De Maleische Handschriften in het Britisch Museum. In: *Bijdragen, Koninklijk Instituut voor Taal-, Land- en Volken-Kunde.* Serie 3, Dl. 6. pp. 96–101. The Hague 1971.

24 Malay items of the Crawfurd collection.

*Catalogue of manuscripts in Indonesian languages in the British Museum.* Typescript draft by M. C. Ricklefs and P. Voorhoeve. 1972. pp. 62. Describes all the Malay items.

**For printed books, see:**

*Card catalogue of Malay books.* About 3000 items, including about 1000 items in Indonesian acquired before 1950.

**For periodicals, see:**

*Periodical publications and newspapers: Malay and Indonesian.* Typescript by R. Aboe Hasan. 1970. Describes about 350 items.

## MON
*MSS. 8. PB 50.*
**For manuscripts, see:**
*Handlist of the Tai and Mon-Khmer manuscripts in the British Museum, to-gether with Pali manuscripts from the corresponding region, and a short bibliography.* Typescript by G. E. Marrison. 1968. pp. 30. Lists the 8 Mon items.
*Catalogue of mainland South East Asia manuscripts in the British Library.* In preparation by P. M. Herbert, G. E. Marrison and H. Ginsburg. Full descriptions of the 8 Mon manuscripts.

## PHILIPPINE LANGUAGES
*PB about 800.*
About 20 of the languages of the Philippines are represented. Separate card catalogues: *see* INDEX OF LANGUAGES.

## SHAN
*MSS. 13 ; PB 200.*
**For manuscripts, see:**
*Handlist of the Tai and Mon-Khmer manuscripts in the British Museum, to-gether with Pali manuscripts from the corresponding region, and a short bibliography.* Typescript by G. E. Marrison. 1968. pp. 30. Lists the 13 Shan items.
*Catalogue of mainland South East Asia manuscripts in the British Library.* In preparation by P. M. Herbert, G. E. Marrison and H. Ginsburg. Full descriptions of the 13 Shan items.
**For printed books, see:**
*Card catalogue of Shan books.* About 200 items.

## SUNDANESE
*MSS. 2 ; PB about 200.*
A few of the printed books are in Sundanese script, mainly legends and folk-lore.
**For manuscripts, see:**
*Indonesian manuscripts in the British Museum.* Typescript by P. Voorhoeve. 1950–54. pp. 15. Notes Or. 6622.
*Catalogue of manuscripts in Indonesian languages in the British Museum.* Type-script draft by M. C. Ricklefs and P. Voorhoeve. 1972. pp. 62. Includes Add. 12340, which was previously listed under Javanese manuscripts.
**For printed books, see:**
*Card catalogue of Sundanese books.* About 200 items.

## THAI
*MSS. 36 ; PB 1200.*
The printed books include many early and rare editions.
**For manuscripts, see:**
*Handlist of the Tai and Mon-Khmer manuscripts in the British Museum, to-*

*gether with Pali manuscripts from the corresponding region, and a short bibliography.* Typescript by G. E. Marrison. 1968. pp. 30. Lists most of the Thai items.

*Catalogue of mainland South East Asia manuscripts in the British Library.* In preparation by P. M. Herbert, G. E. Marrison and H. Ginsburg. Full descriptions of the 36 Thai items.

**See also:**

*Sangsinchai Klōn Suat.* Published by the Ministry of Education of Thailand, Bangkok. An anonymous poem. This edition was substantially based on manuscripts in the Department's collection.

**For printed books, see:**

*Card catalogue of Thai books.* About 1200 items.

## VIETNAMESE

*MSS. 3; PB 800.*

**For manuscripts, see:**

*Classed inventory.* Lists Or. 8218, a composite manuscript including plays, legends, poems and Buddhist prayers; Or. 11683, a treaty; and Or. 11682, a map.

**For printed books, see:**

*Card catalogue of Vietnamese books.* 600 items, including some items on microfilm.

## OTHER INDONESIAN LANGUAGES

*MS. 1; PB 1500*

In addition to the items in the Indonesian languages described above, the Department also has 1500 books in about 60 other languages of the Indonesian family including Malagasy and Oceanic languages. There are separate card catalogues for each language. There is one Malagasy manuscript (Add. 18141). For references to individual languages, *see* INDEX OF LANGUAGES.

## OTHER LANGUAGES OF MAINLAND SOUTH EAST ASIA

In addition to the items in the languages described above, the Department has a few printed books and manuscripts in other languages of mainland South East Asia. For references to individual languages, *see* INDEX OF LANGUAGES.

**See:**

*Card catalogue of Minority Languages of Mainland South East Asia.* Includes separate sections for each language.

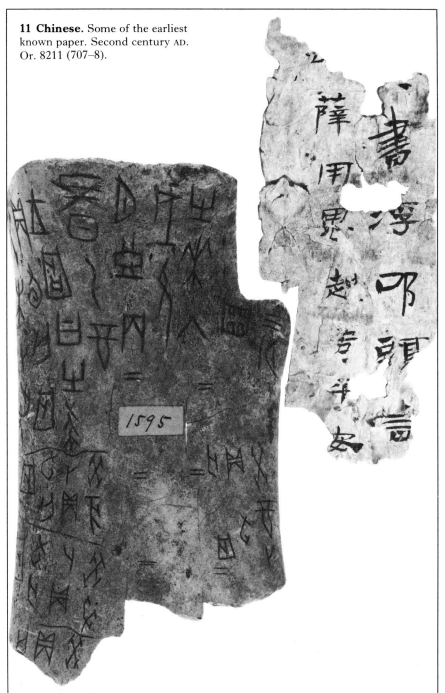

**11 Chinese.** Some of the earliest known paper. Second century AD. Or. 8211 (707–8).

**12 Chinese.** Oracle bone in seal script. Second millennium BC. Or. 7694 (1595).

# Far East

**CHINESE**

*MSS. Many thousands from the Stein collection and about 600 others ; PB about 60,000.*

A large collection of manuscripts was deposited by the Earl of Aberdeen in 1846. The collection as a whole is strong in maps and charts; early dictionaries and grammars, mainly compiled by the Jesuits; manuscripts from the imperial palace (including 45 *chüan* of the *Yung-lo ta-tien*); illustrated albums; and various official and military documents (especially from the *T'ai-p'ing t'ien-kuo*). The Couling-Chalfant collection of inscribed oracle bones, about 500 items, was purchased in 1930.

Of the items discovered by Sir Aurel Stein on his three expeditions to Central Asia between 1900 and 1915, the Department has about 7000 paper rolls and 6000 fragments from Tunhuang, and 5000 woodslips from other sites, including Buddhist texts and other items relating to the period 100 BC to AD 1000.

The collection of early printed books includes one of the world's earliest dated printed books, the Diamond Sutra of AD 868, the Lei-feng ta scroll of

**13 Chinese.** The opening of the Diamond Sutra, the world's earliest known dated printed document, AD 868. Found at Tunhuang. Or. 8210 (P. 2).

AD 975, about 200 examples of Sung, Yuan and Ming printing, and a fully representative collection from 1644 onwards, including 11,509 volumes of the Morrison collection. Besides a complete copy of the first (1726) edition of the enormous *T'u-shu chi-ch'eng* encyclopaedia, the collection includes the major *tsung-shu : Ssu-pu tsung-k'an, Ssu-pu pei-yao, Tsung-shu chi-ch'eng* and the reprints of the *Ssu-k'u ch'üan-shu.* Of particular importance is a run of the *Ching Pao,* or Peking Gazette, which starts *c.* 1820 and is almost complete for the period 1840–1908.

Current acquisition covers all aspects of China's history and culture, apart from scientific subjects. There are some 2500 periodical titles; the collection is strong in Chinese newspapers and magazines acquired under colonial copyright legislation from Singapore and Malaya.

**For manuscripts, see:**

DOUGLAS, R. K. *Catalogue of Chinese printed books, manuscripts and drawings in the Library of the British Museum.* London 1877. pp. 352.
A separate section on manuscripts describes about 300 items. Separate title indexes for manuscripts and printed books.

DOUGLAS, R. K. *Supplementary catalogue of Chinese books and manuscripts in the British Museum.* London 1903. pp. 228.
Entries for manuscripts are incorporated among the entries for printed books. With an index of titles.

*Catalogue of Chinese manuscripts in the British Museum.* Written in 1854 by A. Prevost. In manuscript [Or. 11,623]. ff. 74. Full description of 198 manuscripts.

*Classed inventory.* Includes the only comprehensive list of the 600 manuscripts which are not part of the Stein collection.

*Card catalogue of Chinese printed books.* About 150 manuscript items are incorporated among the entries for printed books.

**For the Stein collection, see:**
**First expedition, 1900–01. (Or. 8211/1-3326).**
STEIN, M. A. *Ancient Khotan.* Oxford 1907. 2 vols.
CHAVANNES, E. *Les documents chinois découverts par Aurel Stein dans les sables du Turkestan oriental,* publiés et traduits par Édouard Chavannes. Oxford 1913. pp. 255; pl. 37.
Describes 991 of the items found during the first expedition, namely Or. 8211/1-991. Uncatalogued Chinese material is placed at Or. 8211/992-1351 and 1683-3326.

**Second expedition, 1906–08. (Or. 8210/S. 1-11297 & Or. 8210/P. 1-20).**
STEIN, M. A. *Serindia.* Oxford 1921. 5 vols.
GILES, L. *Descriptive catalogue of the Chinese manuscripts from Tunhuang in the British Museum.* London 1957. pp. 359.
Describes Or. 8210/S. 1-6980 (manuscript items) and Or. 8210/P. 1-20 (printed documents).
GRINSTEAD, E. D. *Title index to the Descriptive catalogue of the Chinese manuscripts from Tunhuang in the British Museum.* London 1963. pp. 410.
Chinese titles of the texts, which are not all included in Giles' index.
*Card index of works relating to the Tunhuang discoveries.* Includes works relat-

ing to material now in the Department as well as in Paris, Leningrad,
Peking, Kyoto and Tunhuang itself.

*Stein supplement file.* Typescript. Describes the items so far identified from
among the 4000-odd Tunhuang fragments not catalogued by Giles.

### Third expedition, 1913–15. (Or. 8212/1-1927).

STEIN, M. A. *Innermost Asia.* Oxford 1928. 4 vols.

MASPERO, H., ed. *Les documents chinois de la troisième expédition de Sir Aurel
Stein en Asie centrale.* London 1953. pp. 269; pl. 40.

Describes 607 items, namely Or. 8212/200-855. On his third expedition,
Stein revisited Tunhuang and obtained a further 570 manuscripts; these
are incorporated in the Or. 8210 sequence and are described in Giles'
catalogue.

*Les documents chinois de la troisième expédition de Sir Aurel Stein en Asie cen-
trale,* ed. H. Maspero. Non-catalogued items. Typescript. pp. 8.

Brief descriptions of the Chinese items not described by Maspero.

*Preliminary list of manuscripts in languages of Central Asia and Sanskrit, from
the collections made by Sir Marc Aurel Stein, K.C.I.E.* Typescript by L. D.
Barnett. pp. 18. Includes references to 58 Chinese and partly-Chinese
items in the series Or. 8212/1-195. The following other languages are
represented: Sanskrit (various documents and fragments); Prakrit (1 roll);
Tibetan (various documents and fragments); Soghdian (35 items);
Khotanese (1 item); Kuchean (1 item); Kök Turkish (6 items); Uygur
(60 items).

## General

*Stein expeditions archaeological numbering related to OPB MS. numbers.* Typescript. pp. 48.

*Stein collection: table relating expeditions, Or. MSS. numbers, type of material,
and catalogues, etc.* Typescript 1974. pp. 2.

### For printed books, see:

DOUGLAS, R. K. *Catalogue of Chinese printed books, manuscripts and drawings
in the Library of the British Museum.* London 1877. pp. 352.

DOUGLAS, R. K. *Supplementary catalogue of Chinese books and manuscripts in
the British Museum.* London 1903. pp. 228.

*Chinese accessions.* Title index. By L. Giles. Typescript 1931. 2 vols.

*Chinese accessions.* Subject index. By L. Giles. Typescript 1931. pp. 317.

*Card catalogue of the Chinese collection.* About 60,000 manuscript and printed
items. Supersedes all the above catalogues of printed books. The Wade–
Giles romanization was used for works catalogued up to 1966; thereafter
Pinyin has been used. The cards in each romanization are in separate
drawers. With indexes of titles and of subjects.

*Catalogue of rare Chinese books in the British Library.* In preparation.

### For items on microfilm, see:

GRINSTEAD, E. D., ed. *Chinese periodicals in British libraries, Handlist No. 3.*
London 1969. pp. 80.

### For periodicals, see:

*Chinese periodicals in British libraries, Handlist No. 1.* Typescript edited by
E. D. Grinstead, *c.* 1963. pp. 54.

GRINSTEAD, E. D., ed. *Chinese periodicals in British libraries, Handlist No. 2.*
   London 1965. pp. 109. 1603 entries.
GRINSTEAD, E. D., ed. *Chinese periodicals in British libraries, Handlist No. 3.*
   London 1969. pp. 80. About 650 entries.
BRUGGER, W., ed. *Chinese periodicals in British libraries, Handlist No. 4.*
   London 1972. pp. 199. About 3000 entries.
*Chinese periodicals holdings and location file.*

## JAPANESE
*MSS. 277; PB about 35,000.*
The collection originated with the 44 printed books and maps assembled in
Japan by the German physician Engelbert Kaempfer in 1691–2; subsequently acquired by Sir Hans Sloane it became part of the foundation collections of the British Museum. The collection was augmented by the purchase
in 1868 of 1088 works in 3441 volumes from Alexander von Siebold, son of
the explorer Philipp Franz von Siebold; by a collection of illustrated books,
gathered by William Anderson, in 1882; an important collection of antiquarian books, including many early blockprints and movable type editions,
from the library of Sir Ernest Satow in 1884; and further acquisitions in
1896 from the latter two sources.

   Since 1955 the collection has been increased from about 7000 to 35,000
volumes. Recent acquisitions include a wide range of modern scholarly works
as well as antiquarian books representing the long history of printing in
Japan. These include five of the Empress Shotoku's 'million charms', printed
between AD 764 and 770; blockprinted books from the twelfth to sixteenth
centuries, and commercial printing of high quality of the seventeenth to nineteenth centuries. The collection is rich in specimens of early printing with
movable type (*c.* 1590–1650); books printed at the Jesuit Mission Press
(1591–1611), and of illustrated novels and delicately printed picture books of
the seventeenth century onwards.
**See:**
DOUGLAS, R. K. *Catalogue of Japanese printed books and manuscripts in the
   Library of the British Museum.* London 1898. pp. 404.
   About 5500 items. With indexes of titles and of subjects.
DOUGLAS, R. K. *Catalogue of Japanese printed books and manuscripts in the
   British Museum acquired during the years 1899–1903.* London 1904. pp. 98.
   About 1200 items. With indexes of titles and of subjects.
*Card catalogue of Japanese printed books acquired since 1904.* Describes about
   15,000 items. Includes revised entries for some of the items acquired before
   1904.
*Blue-slip catalogue of the Engelbert Kaempfer collection.* Compiled by K. B.
   Gardner. 44 items.
*Catalogue of the pre-1700 Japanese printed books in the British Library.* In
   preparation by K. B. Gardner and D. G. Chibbett.
**For manuscripts, see:**
*Blue-slip catalogue of Japanese manuscripts.* In preparation by Y.-Y. Brown.

**14 Japanese.** Lily from a book of block-printed illustrations of flowers by Yamaguchi Soken. Second edition, Kyoto, 1846. 16111. c. 10.

## KOREAN
*MSS. 24; PB about 3000, including blockprints.*
Outstanding among the manuscripts is the encyclopaedia *Tongguk munhon pigo* in 111 volumes, of about 1840. The blockprints include a number of early editions.
**For manuscripts, see:**
*Classed inventory.*
**For printed books, see:**
*Card catalogue of Korean books.* About 1200 items.

## MANCHU
*MSS. 38; 210 blockprints; about 30 facsimile editions; and a small number of works on the study of the Manchu language and people.*
Among the manuscripts is one of the only three copies of the *Han-i araha Sunja hacin-i hergen kamciha Manju gisun-i buleku bithe/Yü-chih Wu-t'i Ch'ing-wen chien,* the dictionary in Manchu, Mongolian, Tibetan, Uygur (East Turki), and Chinese, compiled in the late eighteenth century.
**For manuscripts and blockprints, see:**
*Manchu books and manuscripts in the British Museum.* Typescript by Walter Simon. *c.* 1940. About 200 entries.

SIMON, W., and NELSON, H. G. H. *Manchu books in London : a union catalogue.* London 1977.
**See also:**
*Manchu books in London.* Typescript by E. D. Grinstead. *c.* 1965. pp. 7.
A short title union list of Manchu books in the British Museum, the School of Oriental and African Studies, and the India Office Library.
**For reference works, see:**
*Card catalogue of modern editions of Manchu texts, and of western-language and Japanese works on Manchu.* About 150 items.

## MINOR LANGUAGES OF CHINA
*Note:* Major non-Chinese languages of China, past and present, such as TIBETAN, MANCHU and MONGOLIAN, are listed separately.

Of the Yi group, Moso (Na-khi) and Lolo are most strongly represented. There are 107 of the pictographic Moso manuscripts, and 36 Lolo manuscripts, as well as a few modern printed works on the Yi languages.

Chuang and the Miao-Yao group are represented by a few modern printed works.
**For manuscripts, see:**
*Classed inventory.*

## MONGOLIAN
*MSS. 30 ; PB 500, including 80 blockprints.*
**For manuscripts, see:**
*Classed inventory.*
**For blockprints, see:**
*Mongolian blockprints in British Museum* (Nos. 1–66). Typescript by W. Heissig. pp. 25. 66 items.
**For printed books, see:**
*Card catalogue of Mongolian books.* About 500 items.

## TANGUT
The Stein collection includes some 4000 fragments of Tangut material stemming from the eleventh to thirteenth centuries; of these fragments, which are placed at Or. 12380, about 40 % are printed, and the rest in manuscript; the majority remain to be identified. All the fragments of a printed copy of the *T'ung-yin* homophone dictionary have been assembled into a single volume (Or. 12380/3110).

There is a small collection of works on Tangut, mainly Chinese and Russian; the Department also has the recently published edition of the Tangut *Tripiṭaka.*
**For the Tangut fragments in the Stein collection, see:**
*Hsi-hsia fragments from Stein collection.* Typescript by E. D. Grinstead. *c.* 1965. pp. 30. Lists site number of each of the 3955 fragments.
*Tangut archaeological index : conversion table from K.K. (Kara-khoto) to Or. 12380 numbers.* Typescript by E. D. Grinstead. 1967. pp. 26.
**See also:**
GRINSTEAD, E. D. A general's garden, a twelfth century military work. In:

*British Museum Quarterly*, XXVI (1962), pp. 35–37.
    On Or. 12380/1840.
GRINSTEAD, E. D. Tangut fragments in the British Museum. In: *British Museum Quarterly*, XXIV (1961), pp. 82–87.
    On Or. 12380/2249-2285, 12380/3947 and 12380/1840.
**For modern works, see:**
*Card catalogue for Tangut.* 25 items.

# Index of Languages

References in brackets refer to the following language groups:
(1) **Languages of North East Africa** p. 23
(2) **Iranian languages** p. 35
(3) **Turkic languages** p. 34
(4) **Minor languages of South Asia** pp. 53–4
(5) **Minor languages of mainland South East Asia** p. 61
(6) **Minor languages of Indonesia and
    other Austronesian languages** p. 61
(7) **Philippine languages** p. 60
(8) **Oceanic languages** p. 61